More Than Just French Fries

15 Business Thought Leaders
Share Insights on Franchising Success

First published by Dog Ear Publishing
4011 Vincennes Rd
Indianapolis, IN 46268
www.dogearpublishing.net

ISBN: 978-1-4575-4984-7

This book is printed on acid-free paper.

Printed in the United States of America

Table of Contents

Introduction

by Jania Bailey

I was in the banking industry for a total of 18 years, which gave me an opportunity to see a lot of different types of businesses. I came to understand that, at the end of the day, all businesses have some basic things in common. First and foremost, they need to make a profit. There are different industries with different metrics that go along with them, but if you can figure how cash comes in, how cash goes out and what the margins need to be to make a profit, then you pretty much know everything you need to know about the business. This information has served me well in franchising since all franchises operate differently but ultimately have the same goals.

I knew about FranNet from my days as a regional director for a franchise company because we frequently got leads from them; they were a great source of business for me. Later in my career, I was asked to interview for the position of president and COO of FranNet. That was in 2006. As I look now at how the training I received through banking has continued to play a role in my career, it just goes to show that everything you do in life feeds into your next opportunity.

The purpose of this book is to provide additional education and information to people who may be considering going into business. The more information you have, the higher your chances of making good decisions and being successful in your next venture.

Who Will Benefit from This Book?

Anyone who craves knowledge about business, and specifically franchising, will benefit from reading this book. We have managed to tap into some of the premier thought leaders and professionals in this industry. To have them all between the covers of this book is phenomenal. Their knowledge and experience is extremely valuable to anyone who is considering becoming a business owner, and if you are already in business, the wisdom in this book can help you expand and boost your bottom line.

When people think about franchising, they almost always immediately think about fast food, which is a very limited view. I am very excited about this book because I think it will open a lot of people's eyes to what's possible for them. The contributors are all fantastic, caring, giving people that, like myself, want to help others avoid mistakes and instead make informed business decisions.

Contributors to This Book

Ken Yancey is the CEO of SCORE, which is a national organization, partially funded by the Small Business Administration, that provides free coaching and mentoring services to small-business owners. His knowledge of small business and how it drives the overall economic engine of the United States is unbelievable. In his chapter, he explains how SCORE operates and what they bring to the table. I think most people don't realize there's even an organization that offers what SCORE does without charging for it.

Then you've got Rocco Fiorentino, who is head of Benetrends, the most respected funding company that business owners of all types can use. Rocco's background in the franchise industry is very deep. He's been a franchisee, he's been a franchisor and now he heads up a funding company. The information he shares about how to finance, where to go and the types of things to think about before you finance your business is invaluable. People have to realize there's more to obtaining capital than going to the bank; that's not the only option. There are a lot of other ways to put together the resources needed to buy a business.

Nick Powills, without a doubt, is one of the best public relations gurus in our industry. What I like about Nick is that he thinks outside the box. He's not traditional in anything he does. His mantra is, "Let's look at your business, let's look at your unique story, and let's tell that story in a way that will resonate with people." Quite frankly, we'd been told time and time again that FranNet was very difficult to get PR for because of our unique value proposition, so Nick took the time to really learn our business, and he has done a phenomenal job of getting us the kind of coverage that we felt was important to get our name out there so that other people could be aware of us.

George Tinsley is a gem. Anyone who knows George knows that he gives back constantly. George is big about making sure people understand what type of opportunities are out there, and it's our responsibility to go after those opportunities. If you look at George's story, he was a professional basketball player who took his earnings and has converted them into a major business conglomerate. The vast number of franchises he has owned and operated definitely shows that you don't have to have previous franchise experience to be successful. It also shows that once you start with one store, you're halfway to 100 if that's where you choose to be.

Steve Greenbaum is a phenomenal individual with a heart as big as his story. Steve comes from a very humble background. He and a partner started PostNet as a small operation, and they've grown it into an international organization. Steve is one of the brightest minds I've ever been around. To watch how his brain works is a real joy. Steve's story brings the perspective of someone starting a company, franchising the company and expanding it into a huge franchisor.

I'm very proud of our FranNet group, and I will put them up against any organization in our industry in terms of the expertise, the professionalism and the integrity that they bring to the table. Their different perspectives can be beneficial to anyone – from baby boomers looking to supplement their retirement income or to millennials approaching business ownership in the early stages of their lives. When you put it all together, it is an absolutely beautiful, thorough story of the franchise industry.

What to Take Away from This Book
I want readers to assimilate the information in this book and allow it to be helpful as they consider their options. I feel like the majority of people that read this book are going to be at some phase of consideration of business ownership. Maybe you're thinking about getting out of corporate America, or you've recently been laid off.

Use this information, study it, think about it and let it open your eyes. Again, I'm a big believer that the more information we have, the better decisions we can make. Let this book be one of your reference models as you examine your options and consider the next steps in your life journey.

About Jania Bailey

Jania Bailey is the CEO of Fran-Net. Bailey has over 25 years of experience in the banking and franchise industries. She worked for more than eight years, and in several different managerial capacities, with Fantastic Sams International, a hair care franchise. In her last position, she served as the regional manager for Fantastic Sams in Texas. Before that, she oversaw operational support and development for franchisees in a five-state region.

Prior to joining Fantastic Sams, Bailey spent 18 years in the banking industry in the commercial lending and business development areas. She has been a keynote speaker at several national events for organizations such as Skill-Path Seminars and Risk Management Associates. Bailey is the author of "Thriving – The Journey to Success in the Business World," a book that was published in 1995. She also has received numerous industry awards and recognitions including: 1998 recipient of the "Woman of Achievement" from the St. Matthews Business and Professional Women Organization; 1997 recipient of the Louisville Business First "Forty Under Forty" Outstanding Business Leaders; and 1995 recipient of the Bell Award for "Outstanding Volunteerism in the Workplace."

Winning in the Game of Franchising

By: George Tinsley

Having played and coached team sports, I came to understand at a young age that you're going to win some games, and you're going to lose some games. When you lose, you learn how to improve for the next game so that you have a better chance at winning. When you win, you must understand that you could lose next time if you don't prepare yourself.

My career in sports was fairly brief, but it was a great opportunity that prepared me for my next step in life. After playing for several professional teams and retiring from the ABA, I started teaching and coaching track and basketball at Male High School in Louisville, Kentucky. During my third year of teaching, coaching and being married, I wanted to be in a better financial position to take care of my family. I was making an annual salary of only about $10,000 at the time, so I started looking for other more financially rewarding opportunities.

I received an offer from Kentucky Fried Chicken as a training instructor because of my teaching background. Because the annual salary provided more financial security and challenge of learning a new discipline, I decided to go work for KFC. It was a complete change going into the private sector, but teaching high school prepared me for developing lesson plans and teaching and mentoring from those plans.

I quickly fell in love with the business. I had an opportunity during those days to actually work with the Colonel himself for three years. Later, I got to go out into the field and work with the franchisees to develop their training and human resource programs. While doing so, I started receiving a number of different offers within and outside the corporate structure of KFC. I decided to take one as an area supervisor for KFC Corporate, in Atlanta where I managed seven restaurants in the inner city market. It was a tough job, but it was an opportunity for me to learn and improve my operations knowledge and leadership skills.

I resigned from KFC Corporate after eight years and became a franchisee of one restaurant in 1984. Over the next several years, we built another restaurant each year. I got up to a total of about 12 KFC stores before I started selling off and diversifying my investments into other restaurant businesses. Now, my focus is both lateral as well as moving forward. All of my experiences in athletics and other areas of my life, both my successes and failures, prepared me to be who I am and do what I do today

Entering the Business World

When I entered into the business world, it was easier for me to develop and study the game plan and understand how to build a team around it. I learned how to evaluate my business on a daily, weekly and monthly basis, which allowed me to fix issues along the way. In athletics, if players are not fitting in, the coach has to replace them. Having gone through the professional ranks of multiple industries, I understand that if you don't perform, you're not going to be around for long.

All of the lessons I learned from sports have affected how I handle myself in corporate environments and as an entrepreneur. Athletics taught me how to perform under stressful situations, how to be humble when dealing with clients and how to listen to others' opinions. All of those were transferable skills that have helped me excel as a business owner.

Can Anybody Be Successful in Business?

I have seen so many brilliant people with business degrees from Stanford, Harvard and other prestigious schools that just haven't been successful in business. Some people do fine for themselves running one or five restaurants, but they may struggle when trying to operate on a larger scale. Then, there are certain individuals who can make 100, 200 or 300 restaurants thrive. It all depends upon their management skills.

Micromanaging is not good managing, if you plan large growth. Being an efficient manager or coach requires being able to delegate and trust your team members to do their jobs. You must allow your crew some range to make their own decisions to attract quality talent, which is not an easy thing. Relinquishing responsibility takes a lot of trust, so you also must be able to evaluate people's performance on a regular basis to make sure that everybody is on the same page.

The Benefits of the Franchise Model

Starting your own business from scratch often requires a large monetary investment in an untested concept with limited research and development around what you're getting into. On the flip side, franchising is a fantastic option for new entrepreneurs because the franchisor has already heavily invested in their concept. They've done the quality controls, they've done the research, they have a marketing team and they are committed to growing their brand. Once you pay the franchise fee, all of those resources are provided. As a potential franchisee, it's up to you to evaluate how good the franchisor is in those various areas to gauge their commitment to their franchisees.

Most new businesses fail within three to five years of opening their doors. But, most franchise stores are still operational well past that mark. Franchisors that have conducted a trade area analysis already have a tested game plan. They've been successful, and they're expanding, so teaming up with a proven franchisor greatly increases your own chances of succeeding.

Mistakes for Future Franchisees to Avoid

I always tell prospective franchisees to do their due diligence. If you're curious about operating a Kentucky Fried Chicken business, go work for free. Get your hands dirty. If you're not willing to clean the restrooms, mop the floor or clean the parking lot at the beginning, you'll never know how it all comes together. You must understand how to order, how to do inventory, how to read your income statements and how to do daily controls. If you've seen all sides of the operation first hand, you won't be blindsided once you've actually got some skin in the game.

In addition to my teaching and coaching experience, one of the things that helped me was working at the corporate level for eight years in different departments. I was able to truly gain an understanding of how the business worked from top to bottom, which gave me a great advantage when I opened my own restaurant.

A lot of new owners are not willing to be hands-on. They want to buy a store and then go on vacation. While that lifestyle may sound appealing, this type of franchise ownership, known as an absentee owner, is a recipe for failure. If that is your objective, absentee ownership, you need to find a partner who is also financially invested to run things, or you're going to have to do it yourself.

The Advantages and Challenges of Self Employment

Operating a business requires a certain temperament. At times, you have to step back and let your employees do their jobs, but you must be willing to make some cold, hard decisions if things are not happening. Sometimes you have to fire people. Sometimes you have to demote people. Sometimes you have family members involved in the business, which adds another layer of emotion and stress that can affect your personal life.

You're going to have rainy days, and you have to be well capitalized to make it through those tough times. You have to be willing to put money away, but you also have to reinvest your profits to buy new equipment, update your building, repave your parking lot and do whatever it takes to stay competitive. If a new highway comes in and redirects traffic, you might need to relocate. There are a lot of business decisions that you will need to be prepared to make and finance, during these hard times.

When you go from the corporate world to being an entrepreneur, you must be able to evaluate yourself on a regular basis. Instead of trying to please a boss while waiting for an annual review, you now have to be a self-starter who is constantly concerned about your own business. You're now protecting your own investment rather than watching someone else's. The measuring stick is a little bit different, but at the end of the day, you're doing it for yourself and your family, which I find to be more rewarding and more exciting than working for someone else.

What Does It Take to Succeed as a Franchisee?

As a franchisee, you have to understand that the franchisor is also your competition in most businesses. Once again, I'll use Kentucky Fried Chicken as an example. If you're a KFC franchisee, you might have 10 or 15 restaurants, but KFC itself has hundreds of corporately-owned restaurants that are competing with you in the same brand.

If the corporate restaurant is not running well, then it's going to reflect on your restaurant and vice versa. Corporations are typically publicly traded, and they're working to increase revenues and profits each year for their shareholders. They have a different business model. They're always trying something different each year to improve those margins, which will inevitably cause changes in the product, production or labor practices. As a franchisee, you have to keep up or make your own business decisions about what is best for your market.

If your store is in the same market as a corporate store, then you're competing against one another. If the franchisor decides they're going to run a "buy one, get another one free" special to grow their sales and draw in more customers, then you, as a franchisee, must follow suit to keep your customers from getting upset and going to the other store.

Before you buy into a franchise, carefully evaluate the franchisor to get a picture of their leadership capabilities. Understand their resources and what their track record has been like since they have been in existence. How many times have they been sued by their franchisees? What happens if your store goes out of business? What if the franchisor goes out of business, or if the corporation merges with another business? Being a successful franchisee may take a lot of time, planning and research, but I think following the franchise model is much easier than going out and starting something on your own.

The Role of the Franchisor

Being part of a high quality, branded concept has certainly helped me during hard times. For example, during the fifth year of running my first restaurant, my building burned down. Had it not been for the franchisor, KFC Corporation, it would have been extremely difficult to recover.

Fortunately, KFC Corporation had developed vehicles to deliver and sell chicken out of, and I was able to develop from that concept. I took a couple of days, followed the lunch trucks that were moving around town and noted their delivery spots. Then I loaded up my truck up with products from another store and drove around selling chicken all day.

Before my restaurant burned down, we were doing right at $1,000,000 annually. When we reopened after developing that trade area with our truck, we made $2,000,000 the following year. Had not it been for the corporation and, of course, my desire and motivation to keep it going, we could have been out of business very quickly.

Advice to Future Franchisees

Franchising is not a good option for everybody. When I tell people that I am a franchisee, the first thing they usually ask is, "How many stores do you have?" I try to get them to understand that bigger isn't always better. Whether you want to have one restaurant or 100 restaurants, whatever your goal is, you must stay involved in your business and not become an absentee owner.

The franchise business is always evolving, so you should take advantage of every opportunity and expose yourself to as much as you can. Go to workshops, go to seminars and meet professionals who have expertise in various fields. Don't limit your options to restaurants. There are franchises in the automotive industry, the home care services industry and even the multi-level marketing industry. A franchising consultant can help you find a good fit for your skill set. The most important thing is knowing yourself. However, you also need that burning desire for success to motivate you to get up earlier, stay later and work a little bit harder than your competition.

All the best,

Mr. T.

"Smile every chance you get. Not because life has been easy, perfect, or exactly as you had anticipated, but because you choose to be happy and grateful for all the good things you do have and all the problems you know that you don't have."

About George Tinsley

George Tinsley Sr.'s road to success could be likened to that of a rags-to-riches story. His is a life story of faith, tenacity, education and a white-hot desire to succeed. George's unyielding determination and strong work ethic are the true gifts that catapulted him to a lifetime of multiple careers, professional achievements, business success and meaningful contributions to improving the lives of others. George William Tinsley grew up in Smoketown, an inner-city neighborhood one mile southeast of downtown Louisville, Ky. Smoketown has been a historically black neighborhood since the Civil War and is the only neighborhood in the city that has had such a continuous presence.

Despite many obstacles, Tinsley capitalized on his athletic gifts and was recruited on scholarship to Kentucky Wesleyan College in 1966, and as a freshman he led the team to the first of three Division II NCAA National Championships. He quickly earned the reputation of being a 'defensive demon', and would take the Panthers on to two national titles in 1968 and 1969, for which he was twice named All-American, selected as an alternate to the 1968 U.S. Olympic Team, and would soon be drafted to the old American Basketball League to play for the Oaks, Washington Capitals, Miami Floridians, Kentucky Colonels and the New York Nets.

Tinsley was already prepared to pursue other options when his three-year tour with the ABA ended in 1972. He graduated from Kentucky Wesleyan on the Dean's List and was the first African-American to receive the prestigious Oak and Ivy Award for academic achievement. Tinsley transitioned his talent for team management to the corporate sector, beginning with an 8-year management career at Kentucky Fried Chicken Corporation where he paved the way to his first franchise in 1984. Within 5 years he had acquired and built 5 more franchises and in 1989 was named KFCC's Premier Operator, the highest honor presented to franchisees. Today, George Tinsley is the President and CEO of PenGeo Inc., Tinsley Family Concessions, Inc., The Tinsley Group, Inc., Tinsley-Bridgeman, LLC, and GW Tinsley Consulting, LLC. His company owns and operates more than 50 franchises in Florida and Kentucky.

After 30 years of entrepreneurship, Tinsley holds as many records in business as he does in basketball. He was honored as KFCC's Premier Operator for a second time in 1994. His KFC restaurant, located in Auburndale has won the KFC Million Dollar Sales Award since 1986. His KFC restaurant has been in the top five sales category, per town size, since 1986. His TGI Friday in Tampa has won the Highest Domestic Franchise Sales award and the Domestic Franchise of the Year award nine straight years.

Tinsley was named Florida's Minority Entrepreneur of the Year in 1989, inducted into the Louisville Male High School Hall of Fame in 1986, inducted into the Smoketown Hall of Fame 1985 and was named Winter Haven Businessman of the year in 2010. He was inducted to the Kentucky Wesleyan Alumni Hall of Fame in 2005, the Kentucky Black Sports Hall of Fame in 2011, the Kentucky Athletic Hall of Fame in 2011, and recently into the Kentucky Wesleyan College Athletic Hall of Fame Inaugural Class of 2013. Tinsley also holds an Honorary Doctorate Degree from Kentucky Wesleyan in Humanities. In 2010 He had the distinction of being the first athlete and African American to give the commencement speech in the school's history.

In the midst of all his success, Tinsley says his greatest treasure is his family. He and his wife of forty-three years, Seretha, have two children, Penni and George, II.

Forget Retirement! Baby-Boomer Franchising is On the Rise

By: Cindy Rayfield

For the past 15 years, I've been my own boss. From a cable company to a bank, I've worked for several different types of companies in the past. During that time, I've always felt compelled to be my own boss. Although I worked hard, I've never felt like I was a good employee. I didn't want to be under someone else's thumb and have my duties or schedule dictated to me. I especially felt that way after I had kids. I didn't just have a desire to spend time with them but also to be there *for* them.

When I was in my 20s, I took the preliminary steps to become a franchise owner. I visited a lovable franchise store in the mall. I thought opening such a business would be easy and that customers would automatically flock to my store. At the time, the franchising process started with filling out a hard copy of the application. I did that, but I didn't get approved by the franchisor. I quickly learned that I lacked the funds and skills to make the franchise work. So, I went back to work while caring for my children.

During my years as an employed worker, I tried to build my own success. I branched out on my own with side projects. I did crafts, freelance writing and website building. It wasn't until I was laid off from my day job that things started to change for me. I was introduced to a new opportunity as a franchising consultant, which took me in a totally different direction in my career. It helped me rekindle my old passion for the idea of franchising and now allows me to be my own boss. I really feel like this is my career version of a Cinderella story. I want to share my experiences with you, and I hope what you learn helps you attain your own fairytale career story.

Downfalls of Retiring as an Employee

To better appreciate the value of franchising as a retirement option, I think we have to first start by looking at what happens when you retire as an employee. When my father retired, they gave him a gold watch and a pat on the back. He did receive a pension, and they covered his insurance. Since he's now in his 70s; and he's risking outliving his retirement savings. Pensions dwindle over time. Today, you're lucky if you get a pension and covered insurance at all.

Plenty of companies are eliminating their insurance coverage for retirees in favor of saving money and only covering their active workforce. We see more buyouts today. Your employer basically offers you a sum of money to leave and hopes the door doesn't hit you and knock you over on your way out. The days of companies being loyal to their loyal employees are over. There isn't even a gold watch anymore. The takeaway point for this topic is that you have to look out for yourself and take charge in building your own future and retirement security.

What Keeps People from Becoming Franchise Owners?

If we know that employers are not loyal, are cutting insurance benefits and are offering buyouts instead of pensions, why are we so inclined to take that route? There are several obstacles that may keep people who are nearing retirement from taking steps to becoming franchise owners.

The initial investment seems like a lot. If you don't have some extra money at your disposal, the investment to become a franchise owner is one of the biggest deterrents. But there are options that many people may not know about, including leveraging retirement funds.

The fear of failing may be high. The fear of failing and losing an investment or part of your retirement money is definitely scary. Fortunately, most people have fears that are overblown when it comes to franchising. By making a smart business choice, following the franchising system and seeking help from experts, you have much more control over your own success.

The time commitment seems too big. This is true. The initial time commitment of starting a franchise is big. The same is true with starting any business, and it's even the same in many jobs if you work for someone else. You're still learning. Fortunately, you can develop a routine. When you build your franchise wisely and start earning more, you may hire a manager and spend less time working. As a franchise owner, you'll still have time to travel, spend time with your family and enjoy your hobbies

Is Franchising Right for You?

I don't want to see anyone dip into their retirement savings and shell out their hard-earned money for a franchise if it's not the right fit for them. My passion is helping people take charge of their success to better enjoy retirement, and I want you to go into retirement with as much security as possible. In determining if franchising is right for you, there are several self-assessment questions to ask.

1. Am I a driver? By this, I don't mean someone who can drive like Mario Andretti. A driver is someone who is perpetually self-driven. You're not afraid to do any kind of work required to make your business succeed. You can roll up your sleeves, work on a task and analyze a problem tirelessly until it is solved. To be driven, you have to have a strong reason for wanting to succeed as a franchise owner. What drives you?

2. Am I ready to make this commitment? If you're not ready to take the first step but you really want to, you have to identify what's stopping you. Do you need to save some more money? Do you want to wait until your youngest child graduates from college next year? There are always a million excuses to *not* do something. If you can't find legitimate reasons to delay ownership, then what is holding you back? If you feel that you are ready but have one or two time-sensitive projects, set a goal for finishing them. Use your time to research, reach out for help and sharpen your skills.

3. Am I an over-entrepreneur? Although franchising is a great option for most entrepreneurs, it may not be the right fit for you if you're *too* entrepreneurial. Do you absolutely have to have

your own rules? Would you be likely to argue with the franchisor about different rules and set methods? Do you find yourself fighting the research process? If you are too independent, franchising isn't necessarily a good solution. You still have rules and metrics to adhere to, and those are determined by the franchisor. Freedom comes from being your own boss and being in charge of your business financials, as well as your own.

Tips for Succeeding as A Franchise Owner in Retirement

Perhaps you want to buy a franchise to fund your own retirement and to leave behind something of value to your heirs. If you feel ready to take that step and have the necessary skills and resources, there are a few tips to remember to help you succeed.

Choose a franchise that works for you. The best thing about the franchising world is that there are plenty of options. You're not limited to just fast food or retail products. What are your marketable business skills? Identify your strengths. Look for franchises that fit your skill set and meet your needs.

Never **deviate from the system.** I can't emphasize this point enough. The system used by your chosen franchisor is designed to help you succeed. If you deviate from it, you can really hurt yourself and your financial future. You're investing in a franchise for the structure it offers. Use that to your advantage.

Remember to advertise. Franchisors will still want you to advertise. You may have to spend a certain amount, and you can often supplement your efforts for your own benefit with free social media pages for your branch. Explore your options, but don't be afraid to invest in your brand through advertising.

When faced with franchising or the workforce, franchising is the stable choice if you pick the right one. Many companies are hesitant to hire older workers these days. Banks are more likely to finance a franchise than an independent business. Also, you have more options than just retail or food with franchising.

There are plenty of reasons to go into franchising as a financial strategy for retirement. What are your reasons? Start thinking about them, talk about them, do your research and reach out to experts for help getting started on your path to a better retirement.

About Cindy Rayfield

Cindy Rayfield is a franchise consultant with FranNet Colorado, offering services to clients Colorado, Wyoming and Montana. She has a history of helping people build and grow their businesses. Since 2001 she has been a business owner, operating a website and copywriting company in Denver that helps small businesses, churches and non-profits with marketing and communication projects.

Diversity in Franchises

By: Jose Torres

One of the greatest things about the United States is its representation of global cultures. In the corporate world, I have had the privilege of working with foreign nationals from several parts of the globe. I was raised in Puerto Rico. I moved to the United States to attend college and grad school before entering the corporate world. Part of my time was spent in the USA, and part of it was spent in Latin America in different high-level positions.

At one point, I decided I wanted to take charge of my career and work for myself. As time passed, I learned that our time and our lives are valuable. I was tired of spending my time and skills making someone else's dream come true. I wanted to start living with the purpose of making my dreams come true.

My next step was starting my own boutique consulting company to help other companies move upward. During that time, I was exposed to the franchise world, and I was hooked. I started to realize the power of this opportunity as I worked with two franchises. As a Hispanic, I especially wanted to help Latinos, and other foreign nationals in my area of South Florida, discover and enter the rewarding world of franchising.

Why Now Is the Time for Hispanics to Enter the Franchising World

Over the past several decades, the Hispanic population in the United States has grown exponentially. It is growing at about five times the rate of the rest of the country's population, and Hispanic business ownership has increased by nearly 40 percent in recent years. The population of immigrants from all over the world is increasing as a whole throughout the country. These are a few good reasons for Hispanics to consider franchising:

1. They already have some valuable insight. Since Hispanics represent the fastest-growing population, who better to serve them than fellow Hispanics? There is a cultural familiarity, and we all know what everyone from our culture likes and doesn't like.

2. There are so many different opportunities. One of the detrimental lessons learned in Latin America is that franchises are all restaurants or retail stores. In most countries throughout the region, that's exactly what franchises are. So, it's natural to move to the United States and think that about all franchises here. However, there are many different opportunities beyond those options. There's automotive, services and much more.

3. They have a natural entrepreneurial spirit. One of the main reasons why people enjoy traveling through Latin America is the huge variety of unique businesses and products. Hispanics are naturally creative and have an instinctive drive to succeed. They look for ways to make money, maximize their ROI and still take the time to enjoy life.

One day working in an independent business in Mexico compared to a day in corporate America is about as opposite as a work day can get. There's not much time to enjoy life in the corporate world. When you're a franchise owner and an entrepreneur, you still have time for your family, fun and relaxation.

Starting from Scratch vs. Moving Forward
According to the International Franchise Association, about 10 percent of the franchising industry is made up of Hispanics. They account for almost 20 percent of the population in the United States. So, you might ask why there are not more Hispanics as franchise owners. This is mostly due to a lack of franchises targeting this eager and capable market, and they don't provide the right educational materials for Hispanics to gain an interest on their own.

In the past, our grandparents and earlier generations believed that you had to build something from scratch if you wanted to be a business owner. It was easier to do then. Today, we are seeing more people who are willing to take an existing concept instead and move forward with it. The advantage of franchising is that you're already part of an established name, and you still get the best benefits of being a business owner.

You already have the right mindset! All you need is the right skill set and resources.

How to Get the Skills
The good thing about Hispanics is their get-up-and-go attitude. They're willing to do what it takes to survive and succeed, and they're not afraid of working hard to get there. This is exactly why franchising is a great choice. These are a few key steps toward getting the right skills.

Start by getting a feel for the business. You can actually develop a strong skill set simply by working in your desired franchise. Start out as an employee. If you work in a clerical job or in a customer service job, you will get a good feel for how things operate. When I say this, I mean working for a branch of the franchise. For example, if you wanted to open a franchise branch someday, you would work for a franchise store near you and not the corporate headquarters of the company.

Study to earn a degree. As a Hispanic, you have many great educational opportunities today. There are scholarships specifically for Hispanics and for Hispanic entrepreneurs. There are government loans and grants as well. Earn a business-related degree to get the knowledge needed to be a successful entrepreneur and franchising star.

Talk to a mentor. Other franchise owners are usually out to help you. Don't fall into the trap of viewing them only as competitors or people who cannot be trusted. Reach out to other franchise owners for help and mentoring. You will be surprised to find that the majority of franchise owners are more than happy to share their knowledge and learning experiences.

How to Get the Resources

One of the biggest hurdles you'll encounter as an aspiring franchise owner is getting the funds to start your business. If you are patient and persistent, you can probably find some grants. Also, there are some other ways to get the resources:

- Involve your family. Another great thing about Hispanics is their strong family bond. In chapter eight of this book, you can learn from Leslie Kuban about the benefits of multigenerational family business ownership. Franchising is a great way to have a family business today. People are going into business with their parents, siblings, aunts, uncles and children. What you get are pooled resources and trustworthy business partners.

- Consider loans or crowdfunding. There are many different types of funding options. Crowdfunding and small business loans are common choices if you don't have a lot of money to invest up front. Talk to a loan officer or financial adviser. The Small Business Administration is also a great resource for finding funding. They help small business owners and aspiring franchise owners get on their feet. Also, the International Franchise Association has special funds for helping minorities buy franchises and pay the required fees.

The Success Stories Are Real

I've had the honor of helping many people who came to the United States from Latin America. I've watched them succeed with automotive, retail, food and service-related franchises. For middle-class Hispanics who immigrated to the United States and are not sure what to do for work, buying a franchise is a good investment. As someone else's employee, your job is never really secure. You can have different odd jobs. However, those are never reliable or steady. If you want stability and the power to make a brighter future for yourself and your family, a franchise can be your ticket to living that dream.

Tips for Success

My passion is seeing foreign nationals succeed in their goals. If you're a first-generation resident in the U.S., you'll have to work harder than citizens who were born here to succeed. If you have the drive to do it, you can if you follow the advice in this book. These essential tips will help you prepare to take that first big step toward franchise ownership:

- Polish your English skills until you are proficient.

- As a new entrepreneur, look for low-risk business opportunities.

- Compare your work skill set to the franchise's required skill set to ensure coherence.

If you're an immigrant with a work visa and want to run a franchise, you need to be prepared to succeed. When a natural-born citizen fails, he can go on to do something else. You must be successful to maintain your visa, your home and your income. This is especially true if your family depends on you. There are resources and tools available to help you succeed. Research, educate yourself and reach out for help.

To succeed, always trust and follow the franchising system.

About Jose Torres

Jose Torres is the Managing Partner with FranNet of South Florida, a leading franchise advisory and development services firm with over 50 offices in North America, Canada and International. Jose has over 20 years of general business management, marketing and sales experience in the consumer goods and services industry.

Prior to joining FranNet, he served as an advisor and investor to early stage companies who franchised their business concepts in the healthy fast casual food and beverage segment. During his career, Jose has held domestic and international senior executive positions in Fortune 500 Firms such as Kraft Foods, Philip Morris and Miller Brewing Company. His areas of expertise include management innovation, entrepreneurship, leadership development, and strategic planning. He now specializes in advising entrepreneurs, executives in transition and investors/startup companies realize the benefits and opportunities that franchising offers.

He provides FREE consultations to individuals, matching their goals for personal, professional and financial achievement with carefully selected national franchise companies. Jose regularly facilitates business acquisition workshops sponsored by the Small Business Administration in Miami, Small Business Development Centers and various nationally recognized private outplacement firms and other organizations.

Jose has an MBA from MIT Sloan School of Management in Cambridge, MA and an undergraduate degree in food marketing and distribution from St. Joseph's University in Philadelphia, PA. He is an active member of the National Society of Hispanic MBAs, Minority Chamber of Commerce, International Franchise Association and volunteer counselor of the Small Business Development Center in South Florida.

The Importance of Values in Building
a High Performance Culture

By: Steve Greenbaum

When my company, PostNet, first got involved in the franchise industry in 1993, it didn't seem like a lot of thought was given to how to make franchise owners feel like they really were part of the bigger picture rather than just being expected to operate according to the franchisor's system. We all want franchisees to follow our system, but we also want them to share our passion, vision and values – especially when it impacts customer satisfaction. Today, franchise companies do a much better job of engaging and inspiring their franchisees through the creation and expression of values and culture.

Why Culture is Key to the Success of a Business

Think of products and services as the body of a business. The heart, or soul, of the business is its culture. A business without a solid culture lacks a soul. Many of us have visited businesses that lack a soul. What you find are uninspired, disinterested people who are going through the motions. You stand in a line for a while, and no one looks up to say, "I'll be right with you, sir or ma'am." When employees are unclear on what the company's culture or values are, customers feel it.

Four Fundamental Values for a Successful Business

Most people today expect values like honesty, integrity, and trust. You hear a lot about them, and you see them on mission, vision or value statements. Those values should be inherent and expected in every business. I like to look at it a little bit differently.

Here are four values that I believe the most successful franchise companies today share:

- Authenticity - People want to know that they're doing business with people who are honest, sincere and genuine. Authenticity cuts through the clutter and builds confidence and trust.

- Purpose - People like to do business with companies that seek to serve a higher purpose or the greater good. For example, our business, PostNet is much more than a printing, marketing and shipping franchise. We help create jobs and support communities by helping local businesses succeed.

- Inclusiveness - People want to be heard, and they want to feel like their opinion matters. Some of the best ideas in franchising have come from franchisees and franchisor team members, because the franchisor took the time to include them in the conversation and to listen.

- Transparency - Whether you are a customer, a team member, a franchisee or the franchisor, everyone likes to know that what they see is what they get. Sharing information, goals or even financials is a great way to illustrate transparency.

Embracing a Brand's Core Values

Most franchises have already adopted a mission, vision and values. Their goal is to identify like-minded, financially qualified people who embrace what the organization is trying to accomplish. For example, at PostNet, one of our core values is "Attitude Plus Execution Equals Performance." You can have a team member that's got a great attitude, yet their skills may be lacking, and no matter how good their attitude is, they are not going to succeed in their role. You can also have an incredibly skilled team member with a less than positive attitude. This value, for us, means that attitude or execution doesn't work well without the other. We hire to that, we train to that and we recruit new franchisees seeking that quality. It's a critical part of our business. In order for values to be embraced, they have to be lived, illustrated through actions and frequently spoken to by everyone in the organization.

The PostNet Difference

We have a lot of competitors that do many of the things we do. The one thing we know we can do better than anyone else is deliver on our brand promise of exceptional service through the expression of our culture and values. You can tell the difference the moment you walk in to a PostNet. It's not just in the way you are greeted but the obvious fact that our franchise owner and their team members are sincerely interested in providing business-enhancing solutions to serve your needs. They'll go the extra mile for you to meet urgent deadlines or solve your business challenges. That's the true expression of the heart or soul of the business, not just the delivery of its products or services.

The Correlation Between Culture, Values and Teamwork

When people feel included, valued and inspired, that can make for a very powerful team. I agree 1000 percent with the concept that no one is above anything in any organization. Even though I am an owner and founder of PostNet, I am prepared to do whatever it takes to get the job done. When the coffee maker runs out here, we all make coffee. Likewise, when I was on season four of Undercover Boss, I can't tell you how much positive feedback I received from our franchise partners seeing me in the center working with customers, handling difficult situations, and really walking in their shoes.

Raising Awareness of Brand Culture and Values in the Workplace

Oftentimes, people buy franchises without understanding that leadership is every bit as important as business operations. Their job is to build, lead and manage their teams and their organization. Franchisees must live, share and communicate their franchise's values and recognize team members who exceed expectations.

There are companies that recognize people who meet or exceed cultural expectations on a regular basis. That can be done with something as simple as a thoughtful personal thank you or in a group or team meeting environment. Recognition can also include gift cards, awards and certificates. No matter how you choose to recognize people, do so in a way that illustrates how that team member exemplified your culture or values and how that positively impacted the business.

Strategies for Employee Recognition

Your team will become more inspired by you getting to know you and you them. By taking the time to learn more about them, you can build lasting relationships that instill your culture and values. It illustrates a sincere desire for that person to know they're valued as a part of your organization. Sometimes I stay away from the gimmicky stuff and really focus on the individual. It's as simple as giving everyday recognition and encouraging team members to speak openly and honestly.

I'll give you an example: I'm a busy CEO, and you are a team member. We say hello in the hallway and I interact with you on a business level, but I really don't know who you are, whether you have kids, where you come from or what your personal challenges are. Now, I turn to you and say, "You know, we really haven't had an opportunity to get to know each other better. Can you join me for lunch this week? I'd love to hear more about you, how things are going and how are you feeling about your personal development with PostNet. I'd also love to hear your thoughts on how we can help you succeed in your role."

I've also learned over my 33-year career that people want to win and be on a winning team. I'm not saying we need to have big wins every day, but it's really important to remember that big wins come from a lot of small wins. It's important to recognize, reward or celebrate the small wins along the way or you may not get the big wins.

Common Challenges for New Franchisees
One of the biggest challenges that new franchisees face is making sure they understand their business or brand's value proposition and can communicate it properly. At the end of the day, why would customers use your company's products or services over the competition? All team members need to be able to answer that question. If you've hired people who have a specific skill set, yet they are not in alignment with your culture and values, it won't work. It never works. The same rule applies for franchisors bringing new franchisees into an organization.

When you look at well-run companies that are extremely consistent with a positive customer experience, it's typically because they regularly talk about their values, train to them and recognize when others exemplify them. Values are just as important as your products or services.

Be The Difference

People want to be a part of something that matters. They want to make a difference and they want to be inspired. If you are considering going into business for yourself, remember to do what you love and love what you do. Do it with people who share your passion, vision and values. And most of all, live those values every day and you will build lasting relationships and a very successful business.

About Steve Greenbaum

As Chief Executive Officer of PostNet, Steve serves as the company's visionary, leading the way for the future with innovative ideas and creative new ways to approach business. PostNet launched in 1992 — the same year as the first commercial web browser — and Steve quickly foresaw the importance of the Internet in PostNet's future and customers' need for high-speed Internet access. PostNet can now help build websites for customers, and we offer online marketing services such as social media management and SEO — all of which provide recurring revenue for franchisees. Steve's vision and business acumen has won respect throughout the franchise industry. He served as chairman of the International Franchise Association in 2008, was named the organization's Entrepreneur of the Year in 2003, and received the Gary Rockwell Award for Excellence in Franchise Development in 2004. Steve was also featured in an episode of the CBS show Undercover Boss in December 2012 (Season 4, Episode 5).

Why Millennials are the Future of Franchising

By: Kenny Rose

My exposure to entrepreneurship came at an early age. From restaurants to a solar company that is currently a leader in Southern California, my father ran a variety of businesses. With a constant reminder in school that a four-year degree was the "only" way to go, I earned a finance degree from San Diego State University in hopes of becoming a financial adviser. I interned at Merrill Lynch. When I say I was one of the youngest employees there, I mean the others had about 20 years on me.

I was really good at what I did. So, why did I leave? I wanted my own success and was hungry for it. I set out on my own as an entrepreneur. However, I don't just desire success for myself. Since I love to help people, I saw franchise ownership as a way for me to help other aspiring franchise owners. Millennials, I encourage you to carefully read the next sections. They're packed with valuable information from my own experiences. You can do this too!

Top Advantages of Being a Young Franchise Owner
In my experience, these are some of the top examples.

1. **Your entire future is in front of you**. An obvious benefit is having a long time to build your brand, reputation and legacy. Nothing is more exciting than watching your business grow and evolve.

2. **You have more energy and determination.** When you're young, you have a long list of dreams and aspirations. If you put all of that energy into making your franchise succeed, your hard work rewards you. Since most people become franchise owners toward the middle or end of their career as a way of securing retirement, they're usually not as determined and energetic as you.

3.   **Your mind can be molded.** You've probably heard people say
     that many employers prefer younger workers who are fresh out
     of college. Why? They can train them easily. Young people are
     still learning and haven't been thoroughly trained. This means
     that they aren't set in their ways, and they haven't developed bad
     habits yet. As a young franchise owner, I know I am easy to
     coach, and that has worked to my benefit.

Common Misconceptions About Franchise Ownership
Millennials often have the same misconceptions about being a franchise owner. If you don't work past them, you go into this venture like
a blindfolded bat flapping around in the dark. Misconceptions are a
big barrier between thinking about becoming a franchise owner and
actually taking the first step.

1.   It's all burgers and fries from here. When some people think of
     franchise owners, they imagine a large corporate restaurant
     chain and a sweaty owner running around to fill in for the per-
     petual staffing shortage. The reality is different. Franchises
     involve much more than food venues, and owners do not have
     to spend 90 hours per week working.

2.   Franchises are all evil corporations. Millennials have grown to
     despise large corporations for the most part. If you prefer to avoid
     global corporations, let out a sigh of relief. Most franchises are
     smaller and help small communities by creating more jobs.

3.   Franchises are like easy turnkey businesses. If people don't pic-
     ture the first scenario, they often believe this instead. Sure, you
     can open a chain store on a busy street and may have success for
     a while. However, you still have competitors and business
     expenses. Running a franchise is like running your own startup.
     If you treat it like that, you're more likely to succeed.

Hindrances to Success
Every business opportunity also comes with obstacles. How you
choose to overcome them makes a huge difference. These are some
examples for young people today:

- Complacency

- Investment

- Skills

- Sales

Job complacency gives you a false sense of security. If you work for a large company, you may assume that your job is secure and your best interest is their priority. Their best interest is *their* priority, and your job security is in their hands. A company can fold at any time. As a franchise owner, you take control of your future.

It takes an investment to start a franchise. If you haven't made a big investment before, you may feel nervous to put down that sum of money whether it's earned or borrowed. The first step is a little scary. Picture your future. What do you see? Your investment is your down payment on that.

If you have a limited or applied skill set that does not involve business ownership, the concept will seem foreign to you at first. With research, support and a drive to succeed, you can overcome that easily.

The concept of being a salesperson may confound you at first. Remember that sales is more than making calls. Since people are coming to you, a major part of your sales is simply building and maintaining good relationships within your community.

Tips for Starting a Franchise
If you feel ready to put your entrepreneurial spirit to work after reading the previous sections, the next issue to consider is actually starting the franchise. I cannot stress enough that you have to go into this process with an open mind and a willingness to amend ideas.

Be personable and good at networking. You have to be able to talk to people if you want to be a successful franchise owner. The wallflowers never get noticed in franchising. Networking skills are a must. Growing and maintaining a business requires both parts of this equation.

Know your limits. In a world of DIY everything, it's easy to feel a false sense of empowerment with new tasks. If your expertise is in one area but you need advice on an unfamiliar topic for your franchise, reach out for help. When it comes to starting and running a franchise, you should never assume. One wrong assumption can lead you down a rabbit hole of destruction and financial loss.

Learn from others' experiences. Think about your vision of a franchise. What you envision will be somewhat different from reality. It might be frustrating or confusing at first. However, you can make your future reality better than your vision. You have to talk to other franchise owners. Ask about their learning experiences, and use those for personal growth.

Don't be an age discriminator. When it comes to hiring employees for your franchise, you may feel intimidated by older people. Remember that you can always learn from your elders, and you can still be a leader to them at the same time.

When you make a follow-up commitment, keep it. Millennials, we have to face the fact that this is not our generation's strength. As a whole, we tend to not follow through with many of our commitments. Following up is especially important when you network with other business owners. You can really hurt your reputation if you don't do what you say you'll do. Even blowing off a few meetings can make a negative difference. Make your plans in advance, and always stick to your word.

Keep your income aspirations realistic. Plan for your future and not just the present. Society tells us to buy everything right now. Pace yourself instead. Always plan for unexpected obstacles, and build from each year's profits. Again, don't be afraid to reach out for expert help. Hire an accountant or financial adviser if necessary.

Taking The First Step

The Small Business Administration's SCORE program allows you to work with experts and mentors for free. No-cost expert advice that is more valuable than a college class costing $1,500 in tuition is an excellent opportunity that no young aspiring franchise owner should miss. The SBA can also help you compare loans and look at financing options.

Also, the Small Business Development Centers of America provides free coaching. If you want to become an entrepreneur or franchise owner but are not sure if you have what it takes, this resource is a great starting point for you.

Are You Ready?

Before you take any steps toward starting a franchise, put your research skills to use. If you thoroughly research of every aspect of franchising, you can avoid common but costly mistakes. We've all been taught to challenge ideas. As you research and connect with other franchise owners, remember to be open and accepting of ideas instead of just challenging them. You have to work on building the perfect mix of challenging and accepting.

Are you tired of going to work and feeling like you're wasting your time and are destined for more? If you want to build that destiny for yourself, franchise ownership may be the right answer for you.

About Kenny Rose

Prior to my work with FranNet, I helped high net worth individuals plan for the future as a Financial Advisor with Merrill Lynch. Although helping business owners maintain and grow their wealth was extremely rewarding, my passion has always been to work with people to accomplish their goals. FranNet allowed me to combine my passion and existing skill set by creating new business owners and building their business portfolios. I received my B.A. in Financial Services from San Diego State University, named one of top ten "Stand Out Financial Planning Schools" in the U.S. by Financial Planning Magazine.

How Franchising Equals Financial Security

By: Pat Deering

During the economic downturn of 2007, the company that I worked for was sold, and my job was eliminated. I had been a corporate human resource executive for decades, but I wasn't ready to retire. It was simultaneously one of the most traumatic and most positive things that ever happened to me because I immediately started looking for something else to do.

Shortly after being laid off, I went to a networking meeting about franchising where a presenter talked about taking skills that you've perfected over the years working for others and applying them to your own business. That's how I bought my first franchise at the age of 57.

The Baby Boomer Business Boom

Many boomers are afraid to invest in businesses because they fear that their time is limited. We hear from a number of different sources that we should be taking it easy and retiring. In general, we don't want to, but society is telling us that's what we should be doing.

Everyone thinks that startups and self-employment are for the young, but it's not true. Here are some statistics that may surprise you:

- According to the AARP, people over age 50 make up 40 percent of those who are self-employed, and over half of those became self-employed after the age of 50.

- People over 55 are the fastest growing group of self-employed workers in the United States.

- The Bureau of Labor Statistics reports that about a quarter of people age 65+ are still working.

- The average lifespan in the United States increases by about one month each year.

When Social Security was first introduced, the average lifespan was in the 60s, so it made sense to retire around that age. However, as you look at how much longer we're living today, we're going to have to rethink retirement and find new ways of supporting ourselves through our golden years.

Franchise = Financial Security
Why is it a good idea to invest in a business or franchise versus hoping for Social Security and income from past employment? Simply put, many baby boomers are not financially prepared for a long retirement period. They haven't saved enough, so they must invest part of their savings to stay secure for another 20 or 30 years.

When you invest in the stock market, you really don't have any control. When you invest in a franchise, *you* are growing your dollars, which many people find more comforting than putting money into a mutual fund where you don't know who is making the decisions.

Buying a Franchise vs. Starting a New Business
There is risk in everything you do when you start a business. However, opening a franchise greatly reduces the risk. Franchisors have operational systems and marketing strategies in place that have already proven to be successful. If you start your business from scratch, you're going to have to pay somebody to help you with those aspects. In a franchise, you not only have the franchisor, but you have the other franchisees that are there to help you. You're truly part of a team.

Other benefits to purchasing a franchise versus starting a new company include:

- You can get up and running faster.

- You are saving money because you're not going through trial and error.

- You have support from others who have a vested interest in your success.

Are You a Good Fit for Franchising?

Successful franchisees usually possess all of the following personality traits:

- They are energetic

- They are outgoing

- They are excited about growing their business

- They believe that failure is not an option

Before choosing a franchise, make sure that you have a clear understanding of what you need to do to be successful. Franchising is not for everybody. For example, if someone is very comfortable sitting in a cubicle somewhere and does not like to communicate, they are going to struggle.

Here are some common mistakes that baby boomers make when going into a franchise:

- They want to follow their passion: Maybe you like to exercise and want to go buy a gym, but do you really know what the owner's role would be?

- They don't talk to other franchisees: Listening, learning and communicating with others is important when running a business.

- They overestimate what they can do with their time and money: If they see someone making X dollars, they assume that they can make more because they just know that they're going to be better.

- They are paralyzed by fear: I frequently hear, "Oh my gosh, how do I do this?" The best way to eliminate fear is through gathering information and data to help you make decisions.

No matter what type of business you have, and no matter what you do, you're going to have days where you lose sales. You're going to have customers and employees that are unhappy with you today, but a good business owner must stay focused on how to improve tomorrow.

Finding the Right Franchise for You: The Importance of Franchising Consultants

When people look for franchises online, they see a lot of names and get excited about what the businesses do. When you work with a consulting firm, they look at *you* first. They help you identify your skill set and determine what you're trying to accomplish to find an ideal fit. Consulting firms can communicate with franchisors to give you information about what they are looking for in a franchisee.

Think about it like this: Would you buy a house without going through a real estate agent? You may save money upfront by eschewing help, but the costs of poor decision-making can come back to haunt you.

I frequently hear clients say, "I would never have looked at that business before," or, "I didn't know that business existed." I'll use myself as an example: When I started looking for a franchise, I had no idea that I could possibly own a business that helps other people find businesses. Unless you have help, you just don't know what's available out there.

Finding Funding for a Franchise

Applying for a franchise is just like borrowing money: You've got to have good credit, or you've got to be a good creditor. If you have too much debt, or you have declared bankruptcy at some point, a franchisor may think twice about trusting you. Many people have money to invest, but there are business loans and other types of funding options available. A consultant can put you in touch with someone to help you with the initial financial planning.

Types of Ownership: Owner Operated vs. Semi-Absentee

There are two main types of franchises: owner-operated, in which the owner is expected to be involved with day-to-day operations, and manager-operated, which is also called semi-absentee because the owner doesn't need to maintain a full-time presence. Semi-absentee options usually include manager-run businesses like hair salons, fitness centers and many storefronts.

Unsurprisingly, most baby boomers find the semi-absentee option to be most appealing; however, the most successful franchises are owner-operated. Fortunately, some franchises let you transition from one model to the other, so be sure to know your options upfront.

The Challenges of Managing a Staff

I don't see many people that haven't managed people in their lives. If you are a parent, then you have managed a household. Whether you have a manager helping you or not, you are ultimately in charge of your business, so you must be comfortable telling people what to do.

Think about what kind of employees you are comfortable hiring, supervising and managing. I often look at my younger clients and say, "What if an employee looks like me, or maybe like your mother? Are you comfortable telling that person what to do?" I sometimes find people that are not comfortable managing service employees, or they are not comfortable managing younger workers. A consultant can help you find a business where you don't have to face those challenges.

The Benefit of Being a Baby Boomer Franchisee

Aside from the financial rewards, owning your own business can be especially invigorating for older individuals. Whether you've retired or have been laid off from a job after years of service, you can't go from being super busy and engaged to doing nothing. I speak from experience. I'm here doing what I'm doing simply because I don't want to wake up with nothing to do. Instead, I get to use my experience and skills to help others.

At some point as a baby boomer, you see a lot of mountains, and you say, "I've already climbed that mountain once or twice." Investing in a business gives us an opportunity to find a new challenge, which keeps us energized and young at heart.

About Patricia Deering

After a long and successful career as a Human Resources executive, I decided it was time to leave Corporate America to become a business owner. I had witnessed firsthand that having a successful career in no way guarantees either job or financial security, and I yearned to be in control of my own destiny and to have the freedom to determine the work/life balance that worked for me. My path to business ownership led me to purchase a franchise by the name of FranNet, a franchise consulting firm. Now, I help others like myself who want to fulfill their dream of business ownership.

Creating an Amazing Client Experience

By: Rocco Fiorentino

I've been in the franchise industry for over 25 years. While I was doing a remodel for a small bagel business, the owner had a heart attack, and he went into the hospital and never came back out. Instead of getting paid to remodel, I ended up with the bagel shop by default. I had to hire some managers because I knew nothing about the business, but you'd be surprised by what you're capable of doing as an entrepreneur even if you don't have the experience so long as you have the passion.

Creating Client Amazement
At my company, Benetrends Financial, we strive to be best in class. If I said to you, "When I talk about theme parks, who is best in class?" you'd probably say Disney World. When you get to Disney World, you already have the expectation to be wowed. They have a tall order to deliver because you're already expecting a high level of service. I'm always amazed at how they manage the massive flow of people before I even get into the park.

At Benetrends, that process starts with our Director of First Impressions up at my reception area. She has to manage customers before they even get into my organization. When people go to Disney World, they absolutely expect Mickey and Minnie to be in costume all day. When I'm at work, I am Mickey or Minnie to every one of those customers, and they expect me to be Mickey and Minnie all day long. I tell my staff that when you walk into this office, remember that all of us do have issues, and they'll be there when work is over. Until then, we have to be on stage while we're here and never allow our customers to notice anything different.

Command and Control vs. Encourage and Inspire
Some entrepreneurs think that the way to lead is from the command post rather than aiming to encourage and inspire their staff. There's a

huge difference between command and control and encourage and inspire. People that you inspire tend to inspire others. Those people that *you* encourage will encourage someone else. If not, all you're doing is giving orders and making sure that you hire the right soldier that can just fill the order. That's not building a company, and it's certainly not building a culture.

Measuring Activity and Impact

Sometimes we don't realize what the impact of our activities really are, nor do we measure it. I have had salespeople get into the activity mode, and they start calling clients while they're driving to the airport saying, "Hey, how are you? I'm flying out to Denver for a big meeting, and I've got a lot of clients to meet, but I wanted to give you a quick call because I know that you had called me, and I wanted to return your call."

If I'm the client, frankly, you just said that you're not good enough for me, and I'm going to fit you in on the way to the airport. I always used to say to my salespeople, "Why are you getting more excited about getting on a plane, going to a show and hoping to get leads while you're not taking care of the leads already in your pipeline? There are people waiting and wanting to close a deal."

I use a simple test to measure the impact of any activity at my business. I simply ask:

1. `How does the activity impact the organization?

2. What resources were required for that activity, and did we really have them on hand, or did we stretch and go outside of our budget to do it?

3. Did it really affect our bottom line?

This formula is especially helpful for people who are personally attached to an activity. For example, I like to go to the franchise business network meetings every month at the Union League. Why do I like to go there? Well, I like the breakfast. I see a lot of my buddies. Now, I have to ask myself what resources are required. I have to take half a day out of my office, drive into town and pay $28 to park. What's the bottom line result?

Well, if I look back at the deals I did or the revenue I generated, none of it came from that meeting. I have to say to myself, I can go there because I like it and consider it time off, but I really can't consider it to be a benefit to the business. When you start to measure the impact of your activities, you'll start to improve your business.

Personal Convictions for Success
Below are some beliefs that new entrepreneurs must have to be successful:

- You must want to make decisions: If you're saying to yourself, "I need to decide what business I'm going to go into," how long would you like to spend doing that? Three weeks? Three months? You need to understand what your timeline is because you don't have three years. If you do, you're not really ready to go into business.

- You must want to be your own boss: Can you really be tough enough to be your own boss? If you're not self-motivated, if you cannot look in the mirror and boss that person around, you shouldn't be going into business.

- You must believe that will is more important than skill: For example, I can probably go into any business and learn about it because I'm disciplined enough with my willpower. I have never, ever fired a salesperson for lack of sales, but I've fired them for lack of effort. If there is no will, the skill really doesn't matter.

Managing Mistakes
As an entrepreneur, I go from one mistake to the next very enthusiastically. Here at Benetrends, we have something called the emergency response team, which is a list of the senior executives responsible for elevated clients. I'm at the top of the list. An elevated client who emails me after they found me on the website as the CEO is basically

saying, "I've got a problem with your organization, and I'm very unhappy."

I immediately get on the phone and call them back within a half-hour, even if it's 10 p.m. at night. I say to them, "First and foremost, I wanted to thank you so much for allowing me to recognize your problem. I'd like to review your file in the morning and give you a call at 9 a.m. or whenever is convenient for you, and I will make sure we correct the problem. Is that okay with you?" The worst thing we can do is mess up an apology with an excuse. I just apologize because it really doesn't matter why it happened, even if it's their fault. What matters is they want recognition, and they want a result.

That's creating client amazement. One of our mission statements here is to make every client a champion. Even if you are a disgruntled client, I can tell you that when we get off the phone, you are going to be a champion of Benetrends because you're going to feel you've been recognized, you've been satisfied and you've allowed us to become a better company. You have ownership in us now. You're going to tell others to use us because even if we screw up, we're going to very well fix it.

Overcoming Barriers to Creating Client Amazement

Often, entrepreneurs just getting started have an ego whether they know it or not. As the vendors come in they say, "I want a better deal." You probably have no right to ask for anything at that point because when you look at it in the scheme of things, you're a very, very small account, and you're requiring a lot of maintenance. Being humble and saying, "I'm new, and I need your help. What are some things we can do to best manage our costs?" is a better way of asking for a discount.

When you're humble to people, their guard goes down. Learn from others who manage people well, whether it's the manager in the restaurant you have dinner at or the manager of the coffee shop you go to every morning. You don't have to go intruding on anyone, but just observe and see what characteristics you can pick up.

Find a mentor who you respect. A lot of us in the industry are very, very giving of our time. If people are willing to ask those they respect in business, they'd be amazed at what others would do for them. Don't be afraid to do that. If you can believe that all of us are smarter than one of us, you will be able to learn from others and certainly teach others after you.

About Rocco Fiorentino

Rocco Fiorentino brings more than 25 years of franchise industry experience as President and CEO of Benetrends. In addition to his role at Benetrends, he is also a Director and Board Member for Swiss Farm Stores and Saxbys Coffee, franchisors of drive-thru grocery stores and coffee shops, respectively. He currently serves on the Board of Directors for the International Franchise Association (IFA) and Chair of IFA's Membership Committee. Fiorentino previously served as president and CEO of Freedom Rings, LLC, an area developer and multi-unit franchisee of Krispy Kreme Doughnuts for Pennsylvania, New Jersey and Delaware. He is a Past Chairman for the Multi-Unit Franchise Conference, and Member and Board of Advisors for the Multi-Unit Franchise Conference. Fiorentino is a frequent speaker and moderator on franchise matters at the International Franchise Association Conference and the Multi-Unit Franchise Conference, and has authored numerous articles on franchise financing. Fiorentino holds a Master of Science in Management from the Richard D. Irwin Graduate School of the American College and holds the distinction of Certified Franchise Executive (CFE) by the Board of Governors of the IFA.

Family Ties

By: Leslie Kuban

My business story started when I was five. My father worked in corporate sales and marketing at the time. When he arrived home one day, I had set up shop with my toys on my baby blanket. I asked him if he wanted to buy some. When he asked me the price of a toy, without hesitation I asked him how much money he had to spend. For him, that moment was a proud one and a good indicator that my apple had fallen from his tree.

Three years later, Dad left his corporate career and bought the first of several franchise businesses that our family would own and grow. Through high school and college, I worked in some of these businesses and at college graduation he invited me to really cut my teeth in business by helping me take over a struggling packaging and shipping franchise. I did just that, turned it around and sold it for a profit. At 25 years old, I had tasted the fruit of equity and enjoyed success largely on my own terms.

I watched my college peers struggle in traditional corporate jobs and I realized I wanted something more. I wanted what my family had when I was a kid. We all ate dinner together, had nice vacations and enjoyed life. If I worked for a corporate giant, I knew I'd probably not have my ideal life. I wanted to earn the income I desired and have control of my time and schedule. So, I knew I wanted to work for myself or build my own success instead of hoping to climb up a shaky corporate ladder before retirement. Thankfully, I am realizing my financial *and* lifestyle goals through family franchise ownership.

What Is a Multigenerational Family Business?
One common and old-fashioned example of a family business that still exists today is funeral homes. Many of their names include "family" or "and sons." Family businesses used to be passed down and preserved through future generations.

Today, parents and children go into business together instead of the parent just starting the business and passing it on to the child.

That's an important part of modern multigenerational businesses. Business owners today want to create something of value for their children and grandchildren. In my case, my father didn't just own one business or have one line of work. He was an entrepreneur who helped me get started. He wanted me to work *with* him and not *for* him, and I was determined to build something of my own eventually.

Baby Boomers and Millennials: What A Team!

These two generations actually make a great team. Boomers who work in the corporate world are nearing their expiration date there, and many younger people today despise the idea of having to give their whole life to their employer. The perfect solution may be to start a family business. The number of family entrepreneurs teaming up together from these generations in recent years has been growing significantly. The parents have the money to start a business and want better ROI to secure their retirement, and they also want to see their children succeed in the future. Millennials are eager to build something of their own in accordance with their values and they, for the most part, have a strong entrepreneurial spirit.

Every Family Business Has Its Struggles

I think we can all admit that we've had hundreds of arguments with our parents over the years. Working with your family *can* be an ideal situation for your future and your finances. However, it comes with struggles that you have to work through and overcome. These are some examples my Dad and I know well having worked together in our business.

- There's a power struggle. The child is the future of the business, and the parent is the authority figure, right? So, who should be in charge? As humans, we have a natural tendency to create a pecking order. If there's one thing entrepreneurs share, it's a passion to take charge. So, this naturally creates a power struggle. In many cases, parents make the larger investments in the business. They may be hesitant to let a child make major decisions and risk losing their hard-earned money.

- There may be respect issues. Family dynamics can be easily triggered when you work together. For example, parents are used to telling their children what to do. When my father and I first worked together, he'd often commit me to do things without discussing with me and without me even knowing about it. I had a big problem with that. Over time, we worked through this but at first it was not pleasant. I became better at communicating this issue with him respectfully and he began honoring my authority over my time and areas of responsibility.

- Other family members may feel left out. When you are starting a business, it's what you eat sleep and breathe. It's what you and your family member and business partners are excited to talk about all the time. Family members not participating in the business may feel neglected, even if it's their choice to not participate. And if they weren't given a choice to be part of the business, there may be jealousy, resentment, and bitterness. They may feel like you're the favorite and take those emotions out on you or others.

Overcoming The Struggles
You can minimize the impact of the struggles and limit their lifespan with some careful planning. As you begin planning your business venture, take these important steps.

1. Talk to other family members. Sit down for a family pow-wow prior to launching the business. Discuss the financial and time commitment realities, who will be involved and to what extent. Allow for a safe, nonjudgmental environment for each person to ask questions, voice concerns and feel heard. Some hurt feelings may be inevitable. If a family member isn't fit to lead the business, perhaps that person can start as an employee in the company and earn more responsibility over time. You should also set

up a succession plan with a lawyer in the unfortunate event that one of you dies suddenly or is disabled.

2. Do a strengths inventory. Make sure you're starting a business that utilizes the unique talents and interests of the participating family members. There are professional strengths inventory tests that aid in making sure each family member is in the right role in the business. Define your similarities and differences and make them a source of strength instead of conflict. Life is so much better when each family member is succeeding in a role they enjoy and feel they have authority within.

3. Set some equality standards. In many cases, the parent puts up the money to start the business. The child puts in more time and work. When power struggles arise, both of these arguments are used for positioning. There has to be a time when they even out. If the goal is for the child to assume more ownership of the business over time, designate specific dates and terms under which this will happen. Put it in writing and stick to the plan.

Also, you should integrate outside parties. An advantage of being part of a franchise is having the franchisor providing metrics and operating standards. These are their rules and not yours, and this can alleviate some of the parent-child friction. Lastly, have an advisory board. This can include a CPA, your attorney, financial advisor or business coach. Consider giving your advisory board some voting capabilities around certain business decisions to assist in working through family stalemates.

Advantages of Multigenerational Businesses
Being part of a multigenerational family business isn't just struggles and hardships. You're spending time with loved family members and are building your own future. There are some major advantages associated with this. For me, these are the top examples.

You build strong trust. Most children who go into business with their parents have a bond with them already, and that bond was built on trust. If you're going into business with an old college friend, you may wonder if your business partner will throw you under the bus someday or run the business into the ground. When there's a strong sense of family trust, you don't have to worry about that.

You build your own legacy. When you run a business together, you come up with your own plan for success. You build it your way, and that's something to be proud of. People in the community see it, and parents can use it as an opportunity to be a good example for their kids. Business ownership can also be a vehicle to build financial wealth and security that the next generation can keep and enjoy.

Yes, you can have fun working together! When you build the business carefully and have those difficult conversations beforehand, a family business can be a wonderful environment. Parents enjoy seeing their children working alongside them. It's a source of tremendous pride and joy for them. I believe I am much closer to my family because of our business than I would have been otherwise. Dad, I know, is thrilled to see me follow in his footsteps and further what we started together years ago.

You'll ultimately have to jump a few hurdles as you start a franchise with a family member. When there's a problem, I suggest using Robert Edward Deming's "Root Cause Analysis" method of asking "why" five levels deep to identify the best solution forward. With determination, a solid advisory team, and choosing the right business at the get-go, you can make your multigenerational family business thrive.

About Leslie Kuban

A FranNet consultant in Atlanta since 1999, my role is to provide education about the franchise world. I assist you with determining if franchise ownership is right for you, and identifying franchise businesses that will offer your best opportunity for success with the lowest risk. I've helped over 350 people successfully transition from corporate life to business ownership. My personal experience as a franchise owner gives me the perspective to help my clients assess their real opportunities, risks, and timing to make sound decisions.

When I graduated from Vanderbilt University, I had already operated family-owned franchises and became a franchise owner in 1996. As the operating partner of Mail Boxes Etc. (now The UPS Store) in Marietta GA, I joined the local support team to assist other MBE franchisees successfully run their businesses. I continue as a franchise owner today as a FranNet franchisee.

I'm an MBA and EMBA program guest lecturer at Emory University, Georgia Tech and Kennesaw State University as well as a founding advisory board member for the Franchising Entrepreneurship program at Georgia State University.

My family's story is a wonderful example of how business ownership through franchising allows for a life of freedom, flexibility and enjoyable work. I look forward to assisting you write your franchise ownership success story. Contact me at lkuban@frannet.com and let's get started!

What Kind of Experience Do You Need to Be a Successful Franchise Owner?

By: Heather Rosen

"Knowing yourself is the beginning of all wisdom" — *Aristotle*

Some people spend a lot of time trying to find out who they are and what they want in life. This is a good thing - to constantly reinvent, contemplate, and revisit until you think you are on the right path - at least at this point in your life, because things will inevitably change and then it's time to reinvent, contemplate and revisit all over again. If you are creative and motivated enough to figure out what path to follow, you should be able to find something that aligns with your strengths and interests. I haven't always known what I have wanted in life, but I have always had a natural drive to identify complex problems and find solutions. So naturally, I spent the first part of my career as a lawyer. I was good at my job and enjoyed it. I used my listening and problem solving skills to help companies make acquisitions, win litigation and come out ahead in contract negotiations, and to help musicians get paid for their art. That part was great, but being an attorney also has an ugly side. On occasion, the work I was asked to do for a company ended up hurting their employees or customers. For example, I spent four months doing mortgage foreclosures for a bank and reading heartbreaking letters every day from people who were about to lose their homes.

The day finally came where I realized I no longer loved what I was doing, and I took a step back and reflected. I then spent several years working on the business side of the legal services industry, and eventually, after doing some career research, I connected with people at FranNet and found out that I could use my skills to help people who are thinking about opening a franchise. It worked! I was happy because I could really help people again, drawing on my legal experience in the business world and my business experience in the legal services industry to share valuable insights and knowledge with aspiring entrepreneurs. Now I enjoy being able to help people solve issues such as "is this the right time to start a business?" and "what sort of business would make sense for me?" And best of all, this business is mine – I am a franchisee myself, so I have the constant support of a team of people, but I have no boss, no office hours, and an unlimited income earning potential. In fact, my business has grown year after year while my time working in the office has decreased year after year.

How did I get here? I don't have a rare skill set, nor did I have an unusual turn of luck. I have just always been open to self-reflection and re-invention, and as a problem identifier and solution seeker, I'm always looking to see whether there are new, better opportunities available. I reflected on where I was and where I wanted to be, identified my own skills and passions, spoke with business advisors, and found a business that allowed me to use my talents in an exciting, professionally fulfilling way, while having the kind of lifestyle I wanted for myself and my family.

Do You Have What It Takes to Operate a Franchise?
You don't have to be an attorney or even have a college degree to run a franchise. What you do need are business skills or at least the ability to learn them, plus patience, and determination.

The skills and knowledge required to succeed in franchising vary between different franchise types. For example, you need confidence and good communication skills if your franchise requires cold calling. If your franchise offers IT support, you need to understand technology and have good customer service skills. If you offer a service to the general population, you need even stronger customer service skills, and if you have employees, even if you have managers, you need to oversee their work, set goals, and understand what everyone is supposed to be doing. Management experience is helpful here. But no matter which business you choose, you absolutely must do these three things:

Listen. Listen carefully to your customers, employees, advisers, the franchisor, and other franchise owners. Dig into what they tell you and follow the franchisor's rules along with the suggestions you get from top franchise owners. Figure out how to adapt their expert tips to your own market. Being a good listener also helps you solve problems. As someone with a passion for resolving issues, my listening skills have been an important part of my overall success.

Research. While you can certainly benefit from seeking an adviser's help when you start a franchise, your research should involve much more than that. Focus on four things. First, look at what franchise opportunities are available in your market and are within your budget. If several good options pop up, look for the one that gives you the highest return on your investment. Second, don't spend more than necessary. Some $50,000 franchises earn just as much or even more than $700,000 franchises. Third, find the franchise that will give you the life you want. Place greater emphasis on looking for a franchise that supports your ideal lifestyle and is professionally rewarding rather than just picking a "fun" product or service. Talk to other franchise owners who have the lifestyle you want and learn from them. Finally, talk with enough franchisees to understand why some are successful and others are not. Every franchise has successes and failures. Look for the franchises where most people succeed, then figure out if you are more similar to the successful ones or those who struggle.

Analyze. Think about why you're attracted to business ownership and franchising. Are you doing it to make a difference in your community? To leave a legacy? To significantly increase your net worth? To sustain or improve the lifestyle of yourself or your family? To help a charitable organization? Will your franchise allow you to achieve these things? Also, think of your franchising journey as a road trip. As you head off toward your destination, you must constantly check your speed, watch for roadblocks and potholes, pass slow-moving vehicles, and check your mirrors to see what's around you. As a business owner, you must identify obstacles quickly and figure out how to surmount them just as quickly. Check regularly to make sure you're on the right path and achieving your goals. Keep in mind that you may need to do extra research and spend some more time consulting with your fellow franchisees to resolve issues. In some instances, you may even need to take a class or talk to a business coach to get back on track.

What Can You Do to Succeed as a Franchise Owner?

Again, skill requirements vary from franchise to franchise. Still, some traits are essential for success in any field. For example, keep these three suggestions in mind as you move toward realizing your business ownership goal:

1. Follow the system. Franchising involves unique systems for operations. Each franchise company has its own operating model, one that has been built, tested, modified, and optimized to ensure you and the franchise succeed. If you don't follow it, you risk failing and losing your investment.

2. Be optimistic. If you get discouraged easily and give up, say, after losing a client or getting a negative response to a marketing pitch, you will have difficulty as a franchise owner. To succeed, you have to be able to handle rejection, bad news, and setbacks. When these things happen, rather than dwell on them, analyze what went wrong and then move forward. If it worked for other franchisees, why didn't it work for you? What can you do to avoid it in the future? How can you make what you're offering more appealing? How can you improve your technique? And perhaps most importantly, is there any chance the client will be ready to say yes in, say, four to six months? In most cases, "no" doesn't mean no - it means "not right now."

3. Be persistent. Persistence goes hand in hand with being optimistic. It is especially important in marketing. You have to keep sending information and putting yourself out there. If you're trying to network with people, you're the one who has to establish communication and build relationships. Don't rely on your franchisor to do that for you. Also, be persistent in following and meeting your business goals.

If you don't trust your own abilities, if you have a tough time trusting your franchisor, or if you tend to give up quickly when things don't go as planned, business ownership is going to be tough for you. When you lack both trust and optimism, you may not be happy with any franchise, even when other franchise owners are happy and successful.

The same will likely be true if you start a business on your own – you will probably find yourself mistrusting employees, customers and vendors and feeling doomed. Successful franchisees and other business owners trust people until they have a reason not to, and see obstacles as challenges that can be overcome.

What Age Groups Are Best for Franchising?
The great part about franchising is its ability to fit into many lifestyles, which makes it a viable option for people of all ages. Take the following age groups, for example. Each has its own attraction to and reasons for pursuing franchising.

20s and 30s: Increasingly, people in their 20s and 30s are interested in franchising for these and other reasons:

- They don't want to be tied 24/7 to someone else's company. They demand work-life balance and predictable, regular quality time with family and friends.

- They like the idea of using their skills and talents to do something meaningful and to make a difference.

- They want their work to reflect their personal values and to do good things in the world. Having their own company gives them a better shot at this.

- They embrace challenges and want more challenging work than what they are doing for their employers.

- They are more confident than previous generations. They feel ready to be the boss, as long as they have the support of a franchisor and a proven system.

40s and 50s: People in this age group also want more time for family. For example, franchising appeals to those who have aging parents or children who will leave the nest soon. It also appeals to those who want to spend more time with friends. And people who want to travel or play a sport while they are still in good physical shape, or pursue a hobby or another passion.

Retirement Age: Individuals nearing retirement may choose to run a franchise after they exit the workforce. Some will choose one while they are still employed - a semi-absentee franchise - and then transition comfortably to an income-producing business when they are ready to leave their day job. With people living longer now, franchising provides a good way to supplement savings and ensure some financial stability by lowering the risk of outliving savings or retirement income.

What Struggles Do Franchise Owners Face?

Sometimes, even people who know they will need a business to achieve their financial, personal and professional goals and who are a good fit for franchise ownership have a tough time getting started. Some people overcome these challenges, but for others, challenges like these will prevent them from ever achieving their goals and living their dreams:

Uncertainty over Income. When you start a franchise, you start with zero customers and build from there. This can be intimidating for someone who is accustomed to receiving a weekly paycheck. But when researching a franchise, you can figure out how much money you will make by asking other franchise owners how much money they pulled out in the first two years, after five years, etc... and you should see a pattern. You can make sure those numbers satisfy your personal needs and financial goals.

Diverting your attention. Once you start your business, starting another business or taking a job will cause you to divert your attention from your business and can even destroy it, especially in the formative years. Most businesses require you to be a full-time owner operator at the beginning. Grow one business at a time. Don't shift your focus to another business or job until you have dependable employees who will allow you to run your franchise on a semi-absentee basis.

Self-doubt. No matter how many people succeed in your franchise, you will likely question your abilities or the strength of your own market. Even after doing months of the diligence, you will have to take a leap of faith. After you jump in, you may find yourself questioning these things every time you hit a bump. To move past this, keep talking to the successful franchisees in your company and avoid commiserating excessively with people who are struggling.

Conflicting Projections. If you do a predictive revenue projection from one franchise location and a cost projection from another, your results will likely be skewed. When you try to project the likely return from your franchise investment, ask at least 10 franchise owners from different markets how much they spend and how much they earn. When you do projections, do not plug in the lowest revenue figures and the highest cost figures. Yes, you want to be conservative, but is lowest revenue/highest cost anyone's reality? Perhaps the franchisees in markets with the highest costs also charge more for products or services and therefore, also see the highest revenue numbers.

What Misconceptions Do People Have about Franchising?
Franchise ownership is not for everyone. Still, you should not summarily dismiss franchising as a possibility because of common assumptions. These assumptions are often the barriers that keep people from living their dream rather than continuing to punch a timecard and be at a boss's mercy every day until they retire. Here are some top misconceptions:

- I'm too old or too young to run a franchise

- It's too expensive to start a franchise

- I don't have enough professional experience or credentials to run a franchise

- Franchising is just burgers and fries or retail businesses with long hours

As an adult, you're never too old or too young to become a franchise owner. I've seen people start franchises in their 20s and in their 60s. There are franchises you can start for around $50,000, and many banks are more willing to finance a franchise than an independent startup. Some franchise models do not require extensive skills or experience, and you don't normally need a college degree to run one. Many franchises do not involve food service or operate out of a retail space, and even with the latter, many retail franchises can be run on a semi-absentee basis. In all cases, though, you *do* have to be persistent and optimistic, be coachable, have some common sense, and possess a willingness to learn constantly.

In closing, I want to reemphasize the importance of talking with other franchise owners and always following the franchise model. Also, don't be shy about reaching out to advisers for help. You could even hire a franchise attorney or a CPA. The US government also offers free business counseling services. Most people are not truly stuck in a rut – they just don't know where to go for help. Take a step back. Re-assessing is encouraged, and reinvention is always OK.

For me, owning a franchise was one of the best moves I ever made. It gave me the joy of being with my daughter when she was little, being with my mother when she was in the hospital out of state, and the ability to experience life to the fullest. For example, I now spend most of the summer traveling overseas with family and friends. It also allowed me to test and practice the skills that I developed early in my career working for other people. I no longer have to ask for time off, beg for a salary increase, or worry about whether I'll get that promotion or if I'll lose my job one day. These are the things I wanted when I made the decision to go into business for myself, and I have never looked back since.

About Heather Rosen

Heather is the President of Fran-Net of Virginia, part of a leading franchise advisory and development services firm with over 50 offices worldwide. She is also an attorney who previously advised small and medium sized businesses including sole proprietors on contractual matters, mergers and acquisitions, litigation strategy, corporate structure, bankruptcy matters, and real estate acquisitions and refinancing. In 2001, Heather became an in-house consultant to large, international law firms based in Washington, DC, advising partners and firm management on strategic planning, client targeting, marketing budget allocation, and proposal writing.

Heather left the legal services industry in 2009 to open FranNet of Virginia, extending FranNet's reach and expanding her family's 15-year-old franchise consulting business.

As a franchise consultant for FranNet, Heather works with clients in Northern, Central and Western Virginia and Washington, DC. She also conducts franchise educational seminars throughout the region. Seminars are conducted in partnership with career transition agencies, Small Business Development Centers, SCORE offices, the US military, and federal, state and county government agencies. Heather is a graduate of Washington University in St. Louis and the Temple University Beasley School of Law.

How a Mentor Can Help You Achieve Success Faster

By: Ken Yancey

In 1993, I became the CEO of SCORE Association, a nonprofit organization that provides mentoring services to entrepreneurs across the U.S. Last year, we helped clients to create 55,000 new businesses and over 61,000 new jobs. What makes SCORE work is our fantastic network of volunteers with amazing experiences who donate their time to assist budding business owners. If you're thinking about pursuing your first business venture, there are a lot of people who are willing to help you.

Why Do Entrepreneurs Need Mentors?
Small business ownership can be a fairly lonely pursuit. You'll likely have a small team of important associates, but you can't go in and discuss your bank line of credit and whether you should try to get it increased or not. Often, you need somebody that you can bounce ideas off of.

Small business owner must wear multiple hats to be successful. Certainly he or she knows his or her trade, but maybe they're not terrific at accounting or at sales or at inventory management or expansion. Bringing in a mentor that complements your strengths can help shore up your weak points. When you're choosing a mentor, one of the things that you must think about is the relationship you have with that individual. Your mentor needs to be somebody that you trust with private details about your financials.

You also need someone who is going to push you and ask tough questions. Sometimes, when you choose friends or family members as mentors, they're not going to press you about payment terms and why you're past due on something or ask you what are you doing to counter a new company on the market that competes directly with you. Good mentors must be willing to contribute and challenge you at all times.

Working On Your Businesses vs. Working in Your Business

In a book series called The E-Myth, Michael Gerber says, "You've got to work *on* your business rather than just *in* your business." Let's say that you own a bakery. If you're working *in* your business, you're making products, you're working on recipes and you're looking at margins and costs.

When you're working *on* your business, you're thinking about where to open your next location. You're asking questions like *Should I open a restaurant that only serves breakfast or a patisserie?"* and *"Should I add something for the evening so that I can extend my hours?* Working *on* your business and working *in* your business are two very different things, but they are equally important for staying profitable.

How to Find a Business Mentor

There are a lot of places where you can find mentors. Certainly SCORE is a great option, and the Small Business Association also has extensive resources. Women's Business Centers run by the SBA are extremely helpful, and you don't have to be a woman to take advantage of them. There are also online mentoring programs like Micro Mentor. You can ask your local chamber of commerce for additional resources or approach successful business people who you've known in the past.

You can ask people in your network, "What are your thoughts on this particular industry?" or "How do you feel about these trends?" Answers to questions like that will give you some insight into how people think about business in general and your business specifically, which can help you to determine the right fit. If someone is a Debbie Downer who only knows how to be critical, you shouldn't choose them as a mentor. On the flip side, if they are someone who thinks everything is always wonderful and great, they are probably not realistic enough to give practical business advice.

You need to make sure that you're getting the right dose of business acumen, seriousness, understanding of the market and willingness to answer questions honestly to push you to new heights. If it doesn't work out for you, you need to remember that the only reason that you have a mentor is to help you. If they're not helping you, they don't want to waste their time either, so find someone else as quickly as possible.

How Mentors Make a Difference

Business mentoring programs like SCORE can provide information, experience and research to help people achieve their business goals. If you're thinking about buying a franchise, a mentor can assist you with thinking through your skills and abilities to pick the right franchisor. Once a decision is made, a mentor can work with you on a feasibility study. Mentors can help you set up your books, find capital and develop a business plan. They might recommend that you go work for another business for a little while to better understand more about how an industry operates.

When you're in a franchise, the franchisor provides you with direction; nonetheless, I still recommend getting a mentor. Not every franchise is McDonald's or Subway or one of the giants. Some of the smaller franchises provide excellent training and product support, but they don't give you everything. Maybe your franchisor didn't teach you all of the ins and outs of HR or how to manage a team. Mentors can fill in the gaps.

Mentors can also read over franchise agreements with you to ensure that you understand everything in the contract, or they can direct you to a consulting firm or someone in a local market that could help you. If you don't understand the accounting side at all, I would encourage you to take some basic accounting courses or at least sit down with a mentor and look at pro forma documents and projections so that you can understand the three primary financial reports that you get when you're keeping books. Make sure that you know when you need real legal help or tax help rather than relying on a mentor or a volunteer. There are some places where you can't afford to make a mistake, and you do need professional help.

When to Seek a Mentor

The best time to seek out a mentor is when you're thinking about starting your business. It's a great time to learn and start asking questions. I recommend that you have a mentor through your entire small business lifespan. SCORE's tagline is "For the Life of Your Business." Be sure to send them a gift basket or something like that around the holidays to make sure they know that they're appreciated. Most of the time, a nice handshake and a warm smile is more than enough for your mentor in terms payment for their services.

When it comes to what it takes to be successful in business, it's not always what you know or who you know; it's who knows *you*. In order for people to know you, you must seek out opportunities to network, which does take time, but it is an investment in your business. You're only one handshake away from your next mentor, customer or business partner, so it's important to make sure that hand gets shaken.

About Ken Yancey

W. Kenneth Yancey, Jr. is one of America's leading experts on driving small business success. During his 23 years (and counting) as CEO of the SCORE Association, Yancey has developed SCORE into one of the most efficient, effective job creation and business formation engines in the nation. SCORE has served more than 10 million existing and aspiring small business owners since inception and helps to create more than 55,000 new businesses and over 45,000 new jobs annually. Yancey empowers and inspires 300 SCORE chapters and 10,000 volunteer mentors across the nation.

Yancey advocates for small business issues before industry leaders and in Congressional testimony. He serves on the Small Business Advisory Council of the U.S. Chamber of Commerce.

As a frequent guest speaker on small business issues and trends in the national media, Yancey has appeared on ABC, NBC, CBS, MSNBC, CNN, CNBC, Fox News and PBS. He is also a recurring guest on several radio shows including Small Business Advocate, Build Your Business, Small Business Trends and Biz Talk. He serves as a member of the HuffPost Small Business Board of Directors and has been honored with numerous awards including 2011 Small Business Influencer Champion, the USA Freedom Corp Award of Excellence, the American Society of Association Executives Summit Award and the Lifetime Achievement Award from the Future of Entrepreneurship Education Summit.

Success Is Where You Least Expect It

By: Blair Nicol

When I was a child, my father told me to *never* become an employee aside from a possible one-time occurrence just to see the internal workings of a business. He told me that when you work for someone else, you're helping them achieve their dreams instead of working on achieving your own. With that as a central education point, he raised me with an entrepreneurial mindset. Almost all of my adult professional career has involved franchising. I first started with a shipping and packaging franchise in Southern California called Mail Boxes Etc., which is now known as the UPS Store. We became the Area Franchisees in Southern CA and also owned two of the most successful locations in the country. That along with many other franchise accolades has helped me become successful in this business format.

Building successful franchises helped me acquire a wealth of knowledge and learning experiences. After that, I wanted to get involved in helping other entrepreneurs achieve their dreams by being an adviser and mentor. I now have the honor of working with a company that allows me to do that and be in a great circle of colleagues who share the same goals. I love helping people find the right franchise for them. What people initially want in a franchise is not always what's right for them, and that's what I want to focus on today.

The Most Common Franchising Misconception

When you think of franchises, what names come to mind? If you named Burger King, McDonald's or Subway, you might have some misconceptions about franchising. Many people also name popular places such as Starbucks, which is actually not a franchise. There are more options than chain restaurants. There are service franchises such as the packaging and shipping chains where I started out. There are over 3,000 different franchises to choose from. The hard part is finding the right one for you.

Knowing your options and doing your research are the two most important preliminary steps.

What You Didn't Know About Franchise Options

You probably won't know about some of these options until you do some in-depth research. Some of today's trends are not what you might think. While food franchises are still the most often purchased category in franchising, there are many others to choose from that may be better suited for you:

- Low-cost business to business companies are more common. These franchises often operate out of small offices or out of a franchise owner's home. If you've never had to use their services, you'd never know about them. The great part about business to business franchises is their affordability. Fewer ongoing expenses and risks make these franchises great choices if you don't have a lot to invest or are not willing to take a bigger risk.

- Light manufacturing is gaining momentum. More people are interested in franchises with light manufacturing. For example, a company that prints signs, posters and other paper-based items can do very well. These companies usually operate in a light industrial park, are traditional Monday through Friday hours, few employees, moderate investment level, etc.

- Semi-absentee franchises are growing. This trend started recently and has taken off in popularity. If you don't want to put in full-time work at your franchise or want time to operate another business, or have a full time job, then this is the structure for you. It still takes work to make these businesses run, and you have to be able to manage and delegate while you're away. These are businesses where you can hire a manager to handle most administrative tasks the day to day operations. We see over 50% of our clients going in this direction right now.

With these factors in mind, the takeaway point to remember is that semi-absentee franchise owners do not buy a business for what it sells or how it matches their skill set but rather for what the business can do for them.

How to Find the Right Franchise the Right Way

When you hear about a franchise failing, it often happens because the owner chose the wrong franchise. Maybe the owner didn't have the time to commit to make the franchise succeed. Perhaps the owner chose a franchise with too many rules and hands-on needs that didn't fit his or her skill set. There are many ways for a franchise to fail because of incompatibility with the owner. I always tell people to treat the initial research process like the process of buying a house. Sit down, think of your needs carefully and make a list. To get started, these are some example questions to ask yourself:

- How many employees do I want?

- What are my goals that I am trying to achieve; professionally, financially and personally

- Do I want to work at home, in an office, in a mall or somewhere else?

- What type of business do I want?

- Do I want to work mostly at the franchise or be a semi-absentee owner?

- What is my skill set, and do I want to use it to work in the franchise?

- What is my budget for starting a franchise?

- Do I want to grow the business into multiple locations?

- How will I grow the business?

- What drives me to succeed in a franchise?

- When I get out of the business someday to retire or move on, what is my exit strategy?

Always create your business model before you start trying to choose a franchise. Otherwise, how will you ever know what you are trying to find in the first place.

Again, the perceived optimal franchise choices for you based on your personal likes may not be ideal for you. Without any research, running a food business may seem like a fun choice. However, a hair salon, a business to business franchise or service related franchise may wind up being better for you based on your business model preferences. When you choose one that requires your presence, insight and work, you have to match it to your skill set. For example, you may want a change from working at a bank and may decide to open a service related franchise instead of picking a low cost service related franchise that is a better fit for your skills. The franchise could end up failing. Owners usually fail because of a lack of required skills or because of improper capitalization.

Go out and talk to other franchisees. Don't just talk to the franchisor. You will really get a feel for what it's like to be a franchisee in certain franchises if you talk to the individual owners. This is one of the most important pieces of advice to follow. What are their struggles? What are the disadvantages? What are the advantages? Are there specific financial hurdles or pitfalls? This is a powerful research tool and should never be replaced by the illusion of search engine magic. When you talk to other owners, you can make connections of your similarities. Maybe you have a similar personality or views that will help you excel in one area. You'll never know until you reach out.

Identifying Obstacles Between You and Your Ideal Franchise
People often fall into some common traps when they're considering a franchise or are taking the first steps of the research process to find one. You have to be aware of the obstacles to better help you identify them as you go. If you don't, you could end up passing up the perfect opportunity or never discovering it.

1. Don't let your peers ambush you. As you talk about the topic with friends or peers, you will hear their opinions. If they're not experts about franchising or are not franchise owners, you shouldn't allow their opinions much weight. Putting aside a potential idea because they heard something or read something can be detrimental to you.

2. Don't get overwhelmed with the initial research. There's no way to downplay the initial research process. It's long and cumbersome. However, it's also very rewarding when you find the perfect franchise. Many people give up when they start the process and realize how much research is involved. As I said before, talk to other owners. It's actually much more fun to have a conversation than it is to read something that you don't know who wrote or posted online.

3. Don't let fear and doubt consume you. When you've finished the research process and have picked a franchise, it's normal to feel some doubt and hesitation about making an investment. If you've done the research and have found the franchise that meets your needs and preferred business model, don't let your fears and doubts cloud your mind to the point of giving up.

You Are the Main Priority
The key idea to remember is that you're buying a franchise for your success, and what the franchise can do *for you* is the most important consideration. You're not buying it for the product or to see what you can do for the franchisor. If you don't care much about the products but the company is a great fit for you, don't be quick to pass it up. People often discover that the perfect fit for them is something completely unexpected. Set your goals, stick to them and find your perfect match.

About Blair Nicol

After a year of working with a globally recognized franchise corporation, Blair soon realized it was once again time to work for him and help others live The American Dream of owning their own business. He is now a Fran-Net franchising consultant for the offices serving Oregon, Washington, Idaho, Alaska, San Diego, and Orange County. He is also one of the 4 principal owners of the Global FranNet Corporation with over 50 offices in North America. He also currently serves as the Vice Chairman of the parent company for FranNet.

Blair graduated from Colorado State University with a degree in Finance and Real Estate. He is also a licensed Real Estate Broker for the state of California as well as he has earned the premier designation in the franchise industry as a Certified Franchise Executive (CFE). He also holds the following awards with FranNet:

2004 Western Regional Office of the Year

2010 Commitment to Excellence - Best office practices

2011 Commitment to Excellence - Best office practices

2011 #3 Top Performing Office in North America

2003-Present FranNet Board Vice Chairman and Pricipal

2014 #2 Top Performing Office in North America

2015 #1 Top Performing Office in North America

He also enjoys golf, fishing, surfing, biking and other outdoor activities with his wife, daughter and son.

Fight for Your Freedom

By: Sarah Brown

My career started as a United States Naval officer on board the USS San Diego AFS 6, which had just opened its doors to women; I was excited and honored to be in the first group of women onboard the ship. I served in the Navy for five years, and although I enjoyed serving in the military, my husband and I decided to make a change since we had spent less than one-fourth of our married lives together. At one point, we walked right past one another on a pier when he returned from a deployment because he didn't recognize me, but we ended up laughing about it later.

After leaving the Navy, I spent some time in the corporate world. I enjoyed the corporate environment, but when my company wanted to relocate me, I wanted to stay. I wanted to build my own future, one that I controlled. I decided to get into franchising for several reasons. When I asked my father for advice before going into the Navy, he told me to keep my head down, work hard, speak up when needed and never underestimate the value of hard work. His advice served me well, and I often relay a similar message to my clients who are interested in franchising.

Success in franchising is about showing up every day and trusting the franchise model.

Many people fall into the trap of thinking that a franchise requires no effort. Someone else established the brand and reputation. People already know about the products or services of popular franchises. Why would anyone need to lift a finger? It's this mindset that gets people into trouble and leads to failure. In franchising, you succeed by working with smart people and putting in a lot of hard work. Also, you can never go against the franchise model. If you do, you risk failure, and you have bought something that you don't intend to use. I equate this to buying a piece of fitness equipment that you never intend to use, although you know that thousands of others have used it with great results.

Similarities of Franchising and The Military

The Navy is a lot like a franchise. Both value attitude and aptitude, and people learn the nuts and bolts of their roles through hands-on work in both worlds. You have to practice until you achieve optimization, and there is a continual need to fine-tune your processes to optimize your team and equipment.

Advantages of Franchising with A Military Background

As people who willingly signed up to serve our country, veterans already possess the main skill for getting into franchising, which is the willingness to take a rational risk. There are several other great skills that work to your advantage in franchising.

- Flexibility takes you far. You have to be flexible to be successful in franchising. When you first start the business, you have to put in a lot of hard work, and your schedule may be scattered until you develop a routine. However, the flexibility learned in the military helps you get over that obstacle. When you get into a routine or make enough to hire a manager to handle most tasks, that flexibility means more time with your family, time to travel and time to pursue your other dreams.

- Staying calm is a must. When you are in a danger zone and are always threatened, you adapt and develop a way to stay calm. Franchising, and small business ownership in general, can be tumultuous at first, and that calmness helps you face any issues that are thrown your way. Sometimes the unexpected happens, and you have to be able to deal with that. I had an experience with an aircraft carrier near my station losing control. Although it was very unlikely to happen, we had conducted drills for such an emergency. When it did happen, I had to stay calm, remember my training and know how to face that situation to avoid disaster. Franchising is similar.

You learn a system that has been proven, and you use it when you face such challenges.

The franchise industry is great for veterans. The International Franchise Association has a program called "VetFran," which educates veterans about the benefits of franchising and gives them incentives. Since veterans excel in this area, over 30 percent of the franchises in the United States participate in the program. The good news with this is that you have a wide variety of industries and specialties to consider when choosing a franchise.

Obstacles of Franchising with A Military Background
While military women and men have the strong skills necessary to succeed as franchise owners because of their military training and experiences, they also face some obstacles that stem from that same valuable training. These are a few examples.

You have a hard time losing the employee mindset. If you spent most of your life in the military and went on to work as an employee somewhere else, your brain is programmed to take orders. Switching to making many of your own decisions can be challenging at first. The franchise model for your chosen franchise still has rules and specific instructions, however, when it comes to delegating tasks to employees and prioritizing activities in your business, the leadership skills learned from the military can help you immensely.

Transitioning to civilian life is hard. This is true for any job or business venture. Your brain is still in survival mode, and all of your body's natural instincts are now being thrown for a shocking loop. You can face this obstacle by reaching out to other military women and men who own franchises. They can help you overcome this, and you should never be afraid to seek help. Approximately one in seven franchise owners are veterans, so take some solace in the fact that your background and skills are transferrable to franchise ownership if you find a good fit for you.

Your roles may change. By this, I don't mean to be redundant about becoming an employer figure or moving to civilian life. If you have a family or a significant other, becoming a franchise owner can change your roles. If your spouse is still in the military, you may be busy working when he or she calls. You may have to find someone to watch your children from time to time if you have kids. You may spend more time away from home, and this can cause several problems. Think about them ahead of time. Talk to your family. In today's world, you can also have a business partnership with your adult family members if that is a workable situation for you. Your family must be supportive of your transition to franchise or business ownership, or you are starting at a disadvantage. My husband has never been involved in the day-to-day operation of either of my businesses, but he is incredibly supportive of the capital we have invested and the time commitment I make to be successful.

Advice for Succeeding in Franchising

One of the challenges of deployments is loneliness. You miss your friends, your family and your life. Although you're back on home soil, you can still get lonely in franchising at times. You may not see your family as much as you did when you were at home or working a regular shift. If you network with other franchise owners and business owners with a military background, you can build a support network and gain valuable knowledge. Loneliness also comes from being the boss, and a lot of higher-ranking senior enlisted and officers experience this coupled with not being able to share the details of your military activities. The military also has clear rules on fraternization and they are for good reasons such as maintaining discipline and not creating conflicts of interest. Owning a business also requires setting clear boundaries, and successful small business owners surround themselves with mentors and professional partners to help them grow their business.

We fight for freedom, and being a franchise owner is a good way to enjoy the freedom of building a better financial future and being your own boss. As I mentioned before, you still have rules and a business design to follow, which is provided by your franchisor, but it is YOUR business. One of the misconceptions about franchising is that you are not a 'true small business owner', and nothing could be further from the truth.   If you buy a Subway franchise (the largest franchise in the world by number of units as of today's writing), then you own a small business, but your business just happens to be a Subway business.

I always tell people to research what they want to do before they jump into it. With franchising, your opportunities range from automotive services to food. Just because food is what most people think of when they think of franchising, you don't have to just open a chain restaurant that specializes in fast food unless you have access to a lot of capital and you enjoy managing high school kids. Explore your options. What matches your skill set? What motivates you?

When you go into this venture prepared, you are more likely to succeed. You have to be willing to stick to the franchise model and work hard. You already developed the necessary skills during your military background, and franchising gives you the opportunity to put them to use for your own benefit.

About Sarah Brown

Prior to becoming a franchise consultant, Sarah was a regional developer for Synergy Home-Care. While there, Sarah worked with FranNet and discovered a passion for helping people realize their dreams of owning a business. After growing the Synergy concept from one location to five in two years, she successfully sold that business and joined us.

Before she was an entrepreneur, Sarah was an executive at Boston Market and a supply chain director for General Mills; Sarah also served in the US Navy for five years.

Sarah has an MBA from the University of Minnesota as well as a BS from the US Naval Academy; she is also a certified Project Management Professional (PMP).

Sarah is active in the Las Vegas community, and has two rescue dogs and a 21-year-old cat. She enjoys reading and taking courses as well as kickboxing and trail running. Sarah also enjoys all of the great shows and restaurants that Vegas has to offer.

Why Businesses Fail and Why You Won't

By: Nick Powills

Think about the last product you bought. Why did you buy it? Another person probably influenced your purchasing decision. Perhaps you saw someone driving a car, picking out a box of cereal or letting out a quiet "ahh" after chomping down on a French fry. People influence your buying behavior. Brands don't sell brands, people do. That's why telling your story is important to growing your business. Let me explain.

Think about your childhood. What did you accomplish and what did you overcome? How have those experiences shaped the entrepreneur you are today? Think about the stories of your past, and then write them down in headline format. This fuel will be essential to you saying yes, you are ready to take control of your next journey.

"Hi, I'm Nick. Nice to meet you," is what we lead with instead of saying, "Hi, I'm Nick. I risked everything and started my own business. To create the fuel, I needed for that business to be successful, I relied on the chip on my shoulder from being called fat, being told I wasn't a good athlete and being told that the chances of me finding greatness would be little to none." We don't share our stories enough even though they can strike a chord and be greatly influential to someone else who has been in the same position.

Why Businesses Fail and Why You Won't Allow That to Happen
How do you pick the brand or idea that best matches your business potential? While it sounds somewhat cliché, pursuing your passion is truly the best option. Why would you put everything on the line and risk it all for a business you don't love? Don't chase dollars, chase your passion.

Your job isn't done once you choose a specific brand or category to focus on; now it's time to start planning for your exit. Are you going to sell or give your business to your children? If you start with the end in mind, you will be able to connect the dots for everything in between.

Talk with as many people as possible. Ask your inner circle what they think about the brand, concept or business idea. If you are buying a franchise, talk with other franchisees so that you can gauge their happiness now that they are in business. If you are really adventurous, ask the franchisor if you can talk with the last franchisee to exit the system. Don't only listen to negative feedback, but try to figure out what that previous owner did wrong and what you will have to do right.

Examine market conditions and your potential profit and loss. Once you figure out how much it will cost for you to be successful, add more cushion on top so that you are already planning for a rainy day. Be prepared for the worst case scenarios so that they don't phase you when they happen.

Stop Wasting Dollars and Bridge the Silos
Whether you own a one-off flower shop or a $500M business, *people* will always be the cornerstone of your growth. The best form of people usage comes from viral word-of-mouth messages, which are something that cannot be forced or purchased. Good brands ask their marketing agency to create a viral video for them. Great brands ask their agency to find stories that revolve around people so that they can create a powerful viral movement.

Take the "Share a Coke" campaign, for example. It naturally gets people to buy more Coke when they see either their name of their friend's name on a can. It also gets them to try different products as they hunt for more names. Through this campaign, Coke enlisted its brand ambassadors to buy more Coke, share more Coke and have more smiles with Coke. It's genius.

Another example is Shake Shack. What does Shake Shack do better than every other burger brand from a flavor standpoint? Probably not much. What does it do to get people talking about its brand? A lot. I remember there was a line out the door the first time I went there, which made me think that their burgers must be incredible. The reality is, they let the 10 people in line do the talking for them by pushing the order line closer to the door. That perception is similar to what Krispy Kreme created a few years back, and it is the magic of getting people to transform your brand.

Market More, Scale More, Become Legendary

Once when I was at a franchisor conference, a franchisee bragged that he didn't spend all of the dollars required on marketing. I looked at him with a puzzled face and asked him how successful he was. He said middle of the pack. I then asked him if he was happy with his business, and he said he had expected much more. I asked him if he gained a return on investment on the money he spent. He said when he spent he made it work. I asked him why he didn't spend the marketing dollars if it worked, and he replied that he didn't have to in order to find success. Needless to say, I remained puzzled.

Failure happens when owners spend their life's savings on a business and decide not to kiss babies and shake hands to make it work. Should you decide to buy a franchise, you are buying into a proven system. If the franchisor says to spend dollars on marketing, then spend dollars on marketing.

Your dollars will need to be stretched as far as possible, especially if you are just starting out as a business owner. The easiest way to make your money last is by connecting marketing silos. That's where PR, advertising, social media and digital marketing become one.

Open up any business magazine. You'll likely see an advertisement for a car company that claims you can drive faster if you buy their latest model. But that same car company doesn't give you a URL for more information, nor do they tell their story. Even though they've spent hundreds of thousands of dollars on the ad, they've missed the boat.

People Sell Brands, People Grow Brands

Make sure every single person in your neighborhood knows you are a local business. For example, food brands can host "pay what you want" days where customers pick their prices, which are then donated to charity. Restaurants can host a day where consumers may eat for free in exchange for a review on any social website or app. It's also helpful to utilize your down hours by having your staff do sampling or coupon drops to area businesses. Do a city block per week, and give every house on that block something free from your brand.

Most marketing plans include direct mail and advertisements in the local penny saver, but they rarely strive to create a sense of community. The benefit of being local is that you can operate your business on a targeted level that the franchisor doesn't have access to. It's why you keep the vast majority of profit in the business as a franchisee.

As you market your story, look for opportunities to include your team and their unique stories as well. Keep an ear open, and find out more about their backgrounds, struggles and successes. Allow their story to become a piece of your puzzle by putting them on menus and brochures. Your staff are a part of your journey.

Business, trade and feature writers are constantly looking for ways to humanize the brands that serve their communities. When your story is validated by a third party media outlet, it's far more cost-effective and authentic than any purchased advertising placements that might attempt to connect the brand with potential investors.

Embrace Your Personal Story
In 1978, Nobutoshi Kihara shook up the world with his creation of the Sony Walkman. He then created the video recorder and the digital camera. He's a genius, yet no one knows who he is. Steve Jobs, on the other hand, is known by everyone for making the iMac, iPod, iPad, iTunes and iPhone. Jobs left the most remarkable impression because Apple made him the visionary and marketing centerpiece behind its products. Brands don't sell brands, people do.

Great stories and businesses always revolve around people. Whether it's Steve Jobs and Apple, Michael Jordan and Nike or Oprah and Harpo, personal ambassadors create great brands. When you decide to take arguably the biggest risk of your career by purchasing a franchise, your personal story will be part of your differentiation. It will be why people connect with you, learn to trust you and give you their hard earned money.

About Nick Powills

Nick Powills, CFE, founded No Limit Agency and its sister company 1851 Franchise in 2008 and serves as Chief Brand Strategist for the Chicago-based firm.

No Limit is a full-service communications agency that establishes and elevates brands by bridging Public Relations, Social Media, Advertising, Digital Production, and a lot of creativity, to best strategize well-rounded and successful campaigns for 50+ clients. By presenting visionary ideas and building real relationships, No Limit is able to create effective media branding strategies to help companies grow. Nick currently leads a staff of writers, media strategists, designers, social media experts and digital producers in an office think-tank where brands are humanized for strong, compelling media stories.

Prior to starting No Limit at the age of 27, Nick spent four years working at a franchise PR agency where he mastered the art of building rapport with media outlets and creating newsworthy pitches for earned media placements. Prior to jumping into PR, Nick worked as a writer at the Northwest Herald, a daily newspaper in Chicago; started Lumino, an online music magazine; and had internships at Rolling Stone and Details Magazine. He holds a Bachelor of Journalism from Drake University in Iowa.

Nick, a native of Oak Park, Illinois, and lives in Chicago with his wife, Sharon and his two children Jagger Wrigley and Lennon Field.

Why Women are a Natural Fit for Franchising

By: Chuck Prenevost

As a business graduate, I started out working for someone else. After a few years, I began to realize that I didn't want to work for someone else. I wanted to be my own boss and live my own dream instead of being a component of someone else's dream. My next step was starting my own service-based business, which I opened in the Toronto, Canada area.

After 21 years of building my business and reputation, the business was ranked second in the city for that service industry segment. I sold the business to my top competitor. It ended up being a good deal financially for me. My competitor's business also benefitted as they inherited the streamlined internal methods and processes that had worked so well for us and which earned my business many awards each year. Our internal business systems and processes were highly efficient and that was the knowledge our competitor desperately needed to maintain their market position.

My wife and I decided to move to the West coast and follow our passion for skiing. We became ski instructors at Whistler Blackcombe Resort in beautiful British Columbia. I took some time off after that to consider what my new direction might be. I got into franchising as my full-time passion to help other franchise owners and entrepreneurs reach their dreams. Since there wasn't as much help available for aspiring franchise owners 30 years ago as there is today, I'm excited to see the positive changes and support mechanisms available today for those who want to take control of their career path and start their own business. In particular, I like to reach out to women and help them see the opportunities in franchising because they are exceptional business owners that don't get enough credit. They are often overlooked by outreach attempts. Networking and building relationships are important parts of helping women succeed.

The most significant consideration of franchising is that it is a highly refined and efficient business system that captures a disproportionate market share relative to that captured by competitors within the same business sector. It is the strength of these business systems that consistently achieves a higher success rate than starting your own business from scratch.

Connecting Women to Franchising

Out of the top ten highest paid executives in corporate America, only one women made the list, illustrating that disparity still exists for women in corporate roles, according to the *Associated Press* May 2015. Some will be motivated by this disparity and be driven to change the statistic while others are driven by more personal goals. Whichever side of the fence you may land on, one of the biggest challenges is the uncertainty of operating a new business venture. Identifying networks such as The League of Extraordinary Women and connecting with other local business owners is an important step for overcoming that uncertainty. To do that, I've learned that you have to have the right mindset and be willing to get out there, talk to people and be the one to build relationships. It is both a short-term and a long-term strategy. It's also a matter of finding compatible networks of entrepreneurs. I always encourage my clients to find network groups with people who are focused business owners and who enjoy helping their peers succeed. You have to build trust just as you would in any other type of relationship.

Women in Franchising Take More Risks

In the past, most of the people I've worked with have been in their 40s or 50s and have been displaced out of the corporate world and generally uncomfortable with taking on the risks associated with becoming a franchise owner. I also observe that clients in their 30s, may still be too hesitant to step out on their own relying heavily on the predictable paycheck from their corporate job. Today, I'm seeing younger and middle-aged women exploring franchising as they seek to take control of their career path. I've also noticed a trend that both Millennials and women have an increasing desire to work for themselves and are against the idea of being a corporate pawn.

Once they understand there are support mechanisms available today and that conducting a thorough research process is critical, they're more willing to take on calculated risks and tap into their entrepreneurial drive instead of working for someone else. Since women tend to naturally be more averse to risks because of instincts, it is harder for them to take those big steps. That's one of the big challenges of getting more women into the franchising world.

Why Women Are Franchising Rock Stars

Women are naturally prepared to become great business owners due to their understanding and ability to identify upcoming trends and what potential niche products or services can earn money.

They are great at multi-tasking, organizing busy schedules to meet goals and have a particular attention to detail. When you combine these extremely valuable skills with their experiences from previous corporate roles, you have a powerful combination that can be leveraged into a new business, setting themselves up for more success. In particular, women have an even temperament. Women are particularly strong nurturers and subsequently tend to look out for their employees and customers. By doing this, they build a strong and dedicated workforce that in turn, provides exceptional customer experiences and loyal clients. This is an important part of their enduring success.

Challenges Women face in Franchising

For women who overcome the aversion to take risks and see franchising as a strong career, there are often still other hurdles on the horizon and this is where I find their natural perseverance helps them navigate such challenges. These are a few top examples.

Entering franchising often requires transitioning. This may not be applicable to all women. As I said before, many younger women who do not have major life commitments are getting into franchising to launch their careers. For those who have families and are considering getting into franchising, spousal/partner support can be a barrier. A spouse/partner may not fully understand the level of commitment required in the early years to launch the business and a discussion or two with them will be necessary to explain what the transition period will look like. In other words, some sacrifices will have to be made early on as part of reaching your business ownership and personal goals. The reality is, once you get past the launch phase, you will typically have more flexibility with your schedule and free time to spend with your family than if you went back to a corporate job.

Choosing an ideal franchise may be hard. Some people have their own ideas of what sounds good, and they often go for that. What sounds good may not always be what is best. For example, I had one client who was an admitted introvert from the IT world. The client didn't want to make cold calls and preferred a franchise targeting the senior demographic market. What I eventually matched this client with, had a market of mostly women of different age groups. After a thorough research process, the client agreed that it was a great match for their skills and went on to become one of the top performers in North America for that franchise system.

The research process takes time. The research involved with finding the right franchise can be cumbersome. I always compare it to shopping for a new car. Most people get excited about the shiny new Porsche in the corner and realize that it is not very practical for that 5-hour road trip with the family. What they need is more like the minivan that you can pack the entire family and all the suitcases into in order to arrive in comfort. You will want to know as much information about the car before buying it and even take it on a test drive just to be sure. With a franchise, it is no different. You have to do research to find out which specific opportunities may be the best fit for you and your needs. Committing to a research process to find the right match will serve you better than any other short term goal you set for yourself.

Treat your research like a nautical adventure. You can see the enticing information on the surface with a snorkel. If you want to learn and see more, you have to instead go on a diving expedition to see what's below the water. Talk to other female franchise owners. Spend some time learning about their mistakes, struggles and successes. Having these conversations will be one of the most important aspects of your research.

Flexibility in Franchising

One of the great things about women is their sense of adventure and their passion for enjoying life. To enjoy life more, you must have flexibility. Franchise ownership gives you a flexibility that does not exist in the corporate world.

In my early discussions with female clients, when asking what was of most importance to them, flexibility came up in the top three. They reiterated that being tied down to traditional corporate work hours was not ideal to maintain the balanced lifestyle they seek and this has evidently become a huge motivation for them.

If you want to devote more time to your franchise, you can do that. You can spend time building client relationships and modifying your methods for success. If you want to spend more time at home and have a flexible schedule, you can hire a manager to oversee the franchise's operations. While your manager maintains the franchise's pre-designed plan for success, you have more time to spend traveling, taking your kids to after-school activities or focusing on your other passions. There are so many possibilities once you perform the research and the initial hard work of getting your franchise going. Here are three great success stories from Franchise.org

http://www.franchise.org/a-tale-of-three-success-stories

Tips for Women Considering Franchising

With their natural abilities that contribute to their success, I love to see women entrepreneurs succeed in franchising and still have time to enjoy their other passions in life. For any woman considering franchising, here are three valuable tips:

1. Learn to embrace risks.

2. If you have a spouse or partner, involve them early on and gain their full support.

3. Ensure you are properly funded from the beginning. If you're underfunded, wait to get started especially if you plan on using your business income for personal use within the first year.

There will be challenges and hard work involved with any business or franchise. If you're ready to become a franchise owner and be your own boss, start networking now to develop your relationships and build a support system that will serve you well into your entrepreneurial future.

About: Chuck Prenevost

With over 21 years as a successful entrepreneur and owner of his service-based business which he started from scratch, Chuck brings a unique perspective to the franchise industry. He developed his business into being recognized as one of the elite service providers in Canada with an annual ROI of 15% - 18%. Chuck knows and understands first-hand, the value of effective business systems and what it takes to start and grow a successful business.

Chuck's extensive management skills include:

- Budgeting and P&L Management

- Sales and Marketing

- Executive-level Negotiations

- Venture Capital Funding

- Human Resource Development

- Operations and Logistics Management

With real world experience, Chuck will work together with you to guide you through your business investigation and match you with successful franchise opportunities that align with your lifestyle and business goals.

Born in Edmonton, growing up in Winnipeg, and having lived in Calgary and Toronto, Chuck now resides in the Vancouver area. He has experienced and gained a vast knowledge of the Western Canadian marketplace while understanding the uniqueness of each province and major city within the country.

Having sold his Toronto-based business in early 2008, Chuck and his wife Esta, moved West, settling just north of Vancouver in the beautiful town of Squamish, BC where they work as ski instructors at the world famous Whistler Blackcomb mountain.